Grace, & Redemption

A Selection of Personal Stories

John R. Searle

Contents

Foreword v

Prologue ix

Part One: Real Stories 1

The Rogue Baby-Minder 3

Love, Joy, Peace 25

How Great Thou Art 39

A Day in Malawi 67

Where Are You Phil? 81

Part Two: Reconstructed Stories from Fact 109

The Renewal 111

The Shipwreck 129

James B. Duffy 143

Foreword

My earliest memory of my twin brother is of sharing a cot with him and engaging in some kind of baby-wrestling match which occasioned both of us to shed our tiny T-shirts. Mother tried to solve the problem by positioning us at either end of the cot instead of side-by-side. My parents told me that we couldn't have been more than about thirteen or fourteen months old when that had happened; but the memory is still clearly with me.

A couple of years later, when we were about two or three years old, my father attempted (so he misguidedly thought), to prepare us to face the big bad world by standing us in opposite corners of the small living room and then, at a given signal, sending us charging at each other to engage in another wrestling match. Discovering what he was up to, our mother was shocked and immediately put a stop to this incipient sibling rivalry. I still remember my father's chagrin at our mother's feminine scruples.

So, we grew up together, apparently born to be competitors. Though twins we were absolute opposites. John was carefree, charming, reckless and the daredevil. He chaffed at any discipline. Whereas I was the conformer to every rule and restraint laid firmly down by our strict parents.

In this brief foreword, I simply want to vouch for the integrity and truthfulness of the very personal and candid accounts of himself that my brother has given, particularly in the two stories, 'The Rogue Baby-Minder', and 'Love, Joy, Peace'. Though his style may be thought by some readers to be florid, even exaggerated, I can offer the firm assurance that John is giving an absolutely accurate and faithful account of his miscreant youth. I lived through it all. We shared a bedroom and I was aware of far more of his rebellious and often outrageous behaviour than he ever realised. But as his twin, I was completely loyal to him and never gave away to anyone the reality of what I knew, however much it vexed and grieved me.

For his part, I am quite sure that my twin saw me as a prig—and I suppose I was. But the heavenly Father had his work of grace to do in me, just as he had to in John. I can never forget when, at the age of forty-seven, I received a letter from him which began, 'My dear long-lost brother...' telling me that at last the 'Hound of Heaven' had caught up with him, cornered him and smothered him with the embraces of Christ's redeeming love. As I tried to read that letter out to the weekly Prayer Gathering of the congregation where I was then serving, I broke down in tears as did many who listened in astonishment and rapt attention.

The story 'A Day in Malawi' gives the reader some small insight into the transformation God wrought in John's life, as does the following story, 'Where are you, Phil?'

A far more detailed account of my twin's life up to his conversion has been given in *Real Lives*, pp 37-99

(D.J. Carswell, Paternoster, 2001, Reprinted 3 times). However, *Grace, Hope, Redemption* covers different ground. The final three stories make interesting reading and, in John's inimitable style, are intended as modern-day parables illustrating the grace of God in unexpected situations. They are based on true accounts of events.

May this little book be an encouragement to those who read it, perhaps spurring some on to pray for loved ones as faithfully as our mother did three times daily for John without flagging from when he left home at age seventeen until Christ found him in his forty-seventh year. *Soli Deo gloria!*

David C. Searle

Prologue

The Old Rocking Chair

The living room of our little council house on the Ashbourne Estate on the outskirts of the city of Bradford was modestly furnished. There was a dark oak sideboard with barley twist legs. In pride of place on the sideboard was a framed photograph of C.T. Studd, erstwhile celebrated all-round cricketer and dashing socialite who forsook a life of fame and luxury to establish an evangelistic mission in the Belgian Congo. Despite the shoddiness of the home-made picture frame there was no denying the commanding dignity which was so evident in the image of Mr C.T. Studd with his flowing beard, bony face and hawkish eyes. His motto was printed below along the border:

> IF JESUS CHRIST BE GOD, AND DIED FOR ME,
> THEN NO SACRIFICE CAN BE TOO GREAT FOR ME
> TO MAKE FOR HIM.

Our father and mother had been co-workers with the great man until God took him away in 1931. Six years later in October 1937, they had returned to the U.K. and although our mother's ill health had prevented her return to Africa and although the mission selection panel had been deaf to her pleading, she determined that she would find her own way back to the land to which, she said, God had called her as a child in Sunday school.

She had a fund of pennies and threepenny bits which were kept hidden in a tin in our pantry.

One afternoon as I came in from school, I caught her counting her little hoard of coppers. They were laid out in piles of one shilling, about four or five neat little stacks. I stared, awestruck at the sight of such riches and blurted out, 'Where did you get all that money?' She swept the coins into a tin and hid them out of sight. 'I'm saving for my ticket to go back to Africa,' she told me. 'Can we come?' I wanted to know. I will never forget the look on her face as she turned and said simply, 'We'll see. The Lord knows. Now, have you learned your Bible verse for today?'

We would eat at a rickety loo table[1] veneered with burr walnut which had begun to bubble and crack. Bits of the satinwood inlay had disappeared, and we sat on bentwood chairs which I suspect were borrowed from a local church. We practised simple tunes on a wheezy old harmonium in order that in coming years we might find our mastery of old 'wheezer' useful to some little gospel cause which was short of a musician.

But by far the scruffiest, yet most cherished and significant piece in our humble little living room, was an ancient rocking chair. It was roughly upholstered in tatty dark green velvet. Most of the springs had escaped from the confines of the frayed webbing giving the seat an ugly, lumpy appearance, but the

---

[1] A loo table was usually round or oval and was designed to be used for those playing the card game of lanterloo.

main function of the chair was not to provide a relaxing couch of ease for our mother. Not at all! You see, it was her 'praying chair'.

As will be seen, untold thousands of lives have been rescued from despair and perdition through the faithful ministry supported by that chair as mother crouched in earnest prayer over the creaking framework, often long into the night, especially when our father was away on a preaching tour. It was during one of these nights of prayer that she said the Lord told her that he had closed the door to Africa and that she would never return. He had another work for her, and she must surrender to his purpose for her life. She later described this painful experience as 'nailing Africa to the cross'. God asked her to trust him as he made her a promise. 'I will send one of your children to Africa in your place. You will need faith and obedience for the new task I have in mind for you.'

We were five of a family at that time and the rocking chair was part of our lives. So, when we moved in 1946 to live in an elegant mansion on the outskirts of Arbroath, I was not surprised when the old rocking chair came along with us. Our splendid new accommodation was to provide a home for missionaries' children, and it was to be run completely by faith. The rocking chair was given a home in the corner of our vast new kitchen.

Alas, over the following seven years I began to resent the routine of church going, prayer meetings and daily Bible verse learning and by the age of sixteen or so I gave up any pretence of trying to live a life which would please either God, my parents or any other nosey Christians who disapproved of me. I began to keep late hours with friends who would have been considered by some to be unwholesome. I quickly became addicted to nicotine and would steal to support my habit.

One morning I arrived home at about 2 a.m. I went into the kitchen for a glass of milk and my eye caught a movement in the corner. It was mother, kneeling at her old rocking chair. I felt a surge of anger and resentment, went over and roughly shook her shoulder. She looked up at me with such love and compassion that I gnashed my teeth in rage.

'What the hell are you playing at?' I demanded.

'I'm praying for you,' she said calmly. Her face seemed to glow like the face of an angel.

'Well, leave me alone!' I shouted furiously. 'I don't want you praying for me.'

She began to push herself to her feet. 'I can go to bed now that I know you're safely home.' She reached out and touched my cheek. 'You'll never stop me praying for you,' she said. 'Goodnight, Johnny Boy.'

* * *

Fifty-five years later I arrived in Malawi, Central Africa to speak at the synod of a group of five hundred African churches.

I had been invited because one of the leaders had visited the village Baptist church which I had pastored for eleven years.

'Would you let your Pastor come to Africa to speak at the synod. I'm asking because he has the Word of God in his bones. There'll be two or three hundred Pastors at the conference, many from poor remote areas who need encouragement. They all enjoy the synod meetings because they know there'll be food for them and a dry bed to sleep on with warm blankets. But it's the ministry of the Word they love best of all.'

* * *

On the night of my arrival, the telephone rang. Abraham, my host, looked bewildered.

'It's a lady, asking for you,' he told me, handing over the receiver.

'Hello, who's this?' I asked, mystified.

A familiar voice said, 'Ahh, is that truly my naughty boy? Is it really you, Johnny Boy? Are you actually in Africa? Praise the dear, faithful Lord! He has kept his Word and sent one of my children to Africa in my place. And Oh, Johnny Boy, that it should be you! I shouldn't doubt, I know, but I keep wondering if I'm dreaming and asking your father to pinch me! Let me tell you what I've written in my diary today. It's from Luke chapter 2 verses 29-30 (NIV): "Sovereign Lord, as you have promised, you now dismiss your servant in peace. For my eyes have seen your salvation, which you have prepared in the sight of all people.'"

Before her death at age ninety-eight years, our mother would live to see the Lord doing immeasurably more than all she could have asked or imagined according to his power that was at work in her as she had wrestled in prayer for interminable hours at that ugly old rocking chair. This little book is a testimony to both the challenges her prayers encountered, followed by accounts of the joy and praise with which God blessed her through his gracious work in her rebellious son.[2]

---

[2] As John's twin, I also experienced her prayers and closeness to God as she knelt at that rocking chair. On one occasion before we moved to Arbroath in Scotland—I could not have been more than four or five years old—I rose early and went downstairs. There she was, kneeling at the rocking chair. She got up from her knees, sat on the rocking chair, lifted me on to her knee and taught me the simple gospel chorus:

> *Into my heart, into my heart,*
> *come into my heart, Lord Jesus;*
> *come in today, come in to stay;*
> *come into my heart, Lord Jesus.*

Then she told me the Lord had told her that John would one day work for him in Africa, and I would work in India. She lived to see me visiting India on five successive years to engage in training pastors in expository preaching.

Part One
Real Stories

The Rogue Baby-Minder

Introduction

It was on a chill, dismal February day in the year 1950 that my infant sister Lizzie who, just a few months short of her first birthday, narrowly escaped serious injury. It was due to a heart stopping accident for which, rather unfairly, I was held to be totally responsible. The implications of my reckless behaviour that day, which may well have resulted in a tragic case of infanticide, cannot be over emphasised. It should be understood that Lizzie had been deemed to be no ordinary child. She was born on the seventh day of the seventh month of '49, figures which would seem to indicate that, since the number seven is generally considered by many to signify divine approval, sister Lizzie was destined to be a child of considerable spiritual significance. Added to this were the unlikely circumstances which brought her into the world. Mother was forty-five years old, not considered to be in ideal health, and Lizzie was what is commonly known as 'unplanned', at least by our parents. As a result, she was cosseted, cherished and jealously protected from the outset of her life, all of which ought to have added to the burden of guilt which I should surely have felt for my foolhardy irresponsibility on that fateful day. For seven decades I have carried the stigma of sole culpability for my baby sister's terrifying brush with death without the benefit of advocacy, but I believe that there is a strong case for mitigation which has never yet been heard.

It is encouraging to remember that in a court of law, as the accused stands already condemned in the dock, proceedings have not quite run their full course and sentence is not usually passed until counsel for the defence has been allowed time to offer mitigating circumstances. This can prove to be an invitation for an eloquent advocate to embark upon a pathetic history of misadventures which have befallen the accused, rendering him a virtually helpless victim of circumstances over which he had no control. In a world where self-justification is rather like the shell into which a hermit crab takes shelter to protect its vulnerability, a touching plea of mitigation can often reduce the severity of a guilty man's sentence. He is not properly absolved, of course! The guilty verdict remains, and he cannot legally be declared innocent. Like the majority of humankind, he can only mitigate his culpability. But he will have to settle for that. After all, he will be obliged to share his penal accommodation with a number of nefarious felons, most of whom, he would insist, are much worse offenders than he is!

Chapter One

MacLasher was not the real name of the teacher who would set an ambush just inside the doors of the South Wing of the High School to which I was sent in the hope of completing my secondary education, but it is a title which perfectly describes his life's controlling passion which was not to impart the mysterious secrets of mathematics to his students, but to inflict agonising pain on as many pupils as he possibly could within the time limits of school hours. Male or female, it made no difference to MacLasher, eleven or eighteen-year olds, all were fair game to him. Just let him catch some wretched pupil straying outside the limits of school rules and regulations and their fate would be sealed. School assembly was one of his favoured hunting grounds, for it was there that he was sure to gather a number of late comers. He would hide out of sight, just behind the open door, waiting for the school bell to summon the school to morning assembly in the hall. Even before the echo of the bell had faded, he would take up his position and stand, stock still, awaiting his prey.

Inevitably two or three would one by one be caught in the predatory web. 'Stand here quietly, behind me,' he'd say in a low voice, not wanting to blow his cover. His miserable little group of miscreants would be herded into a corner behind him to await their terrifying fate. 'Please, sir, my ma's no' weel,' a frail twelve-year old girl might say in a heart rending, plaintive voice. 'Quietly, I said wait there quietly,' MacLasher would warn in a menacing whisper. He had heard most of the excuses before, and even if he hadn't, as with this whimpering little victim, it mattered not to him. 'Please, sir, I had a puncture,' 'Please, sir, I missed the bus,' 'Please, sir I forgot my homework.' But no mitigating circumstance, however unimaginative, compelling or inventive, made a scrap of difference to MacLasher. I knew that from bitter experience. 'Please sir, my dog followed me to school and I had to take him home,' I had offered, when, for the first and only time, I had fallen foul of his ambush. As a startled eleven year old, it had been the best I could do, given the sudden shock of unexpected entrapment, but I may as well not have bothered trying an original excuse for all the difference it made.

Assembly would begin with a hymn. Any important announcements would be followed by the repetition of the Lord's Prayer. The words 'Forever and ever, Amen,' were the signal that there was to be no reprieve for the wretched trophies of MacLasher's morning hunting expedition. No pleading, however earnest, would bring about any change of mind. 'Follow me,' he would order, and the condemned little cluster of offenders would fall in obediently behind him and climb the steps to his classroom, there to receive due punishment for their misdeeds; and were they not for all the world rather like a condemned prisoner who has had no advocate to plead for him, but has yet been subject to the full weight of justice without mercy as the maximum sentence is pronounced and he leaves the court under guard with the words, 'Take him down!' ringing in his ears.

MacLasher was my mitigation for the crime I committed on that horrid day which so endangered the very life of my sister Lizzie. He was one of the only four teachers in the school who owned a Lochgelly belt which was a lethal weapon made exclusively in a dismal little town in Fife. As Liverpool is known for a rock group called the Beatles and Melton Mowbray is renowned for pork pies, so the town of Lochgelly is entitled to its macabre notoriety as the sole source of a disciplinary instrument which wreaked physical and psychological damage upon many in a generation who suffered the agonies of its application in the hands of sadists like MacLasher.

I have heard a number of adults insisting that they actually benefitted from the application of the 'strap' during their schooldays and that physical punishment never harmed anyone. All I can say is that they never encountered MacLasher and his Lochgelly belt. Fashioned from leather especially selected for its stiffness, the Lochgelly was at least a quarter of an inch thick; about an inch and a quarter wide, the business end was divided into three vicious thongs. When MacLasher held his belt behind his shoulder in preparation for a strike, it didn't bend, but stretched out straight behind him as though made of some mysterious slightly flexible material. It was rumoured amongst us that it had been specially treated by a cocktail of chemicals, known only to MacLasher, to increase its performance as a means of delivering maximum agony.

MacLasher enjoyed an audience. He waited until his class was seated quietly before removing the Lochgelly from his desk. The one girl in the hapless little group began to wail. 'My Ma's no' weel,' she cried, 'an' I'm under the doctor!' MacLasher spoke in a soft, level voice as though trying to soothe the distressed girl. 'Just hold out your hand, nice and flat.' The poor victim held up a trembling hand, half closed, like a bird's claw. She was crying uncontrollably, now and then hiccupping loudly as though trying to catch her breath. Unbearable tension swept through the classroom. Girls crouched at their desks, eyes closed, as though praying, while some of the boys glared at one another in indignation, teeth clenched, chests heaving in helpless rage.

MacLasher reached out and took hold of the girl's fingertips. 'Nice and flat,' he whispered, opening her hand. 'Ah, that's better,' he said, staring at the tender shining palm. He took aim and paused for a second. Surely, surely, he would not strike with all his force. He gathered himself and took a deep breath. The Lochgelly hissed down like a striking cobra. The class gasped. The girl shouted in agony. MacLasher took her by the shoulder with one hand and made her stand up straight. He prodded her stomach with the butt of his belt and told her in a gentle, confidential voice to be careful to be on time in future. She wasn't listening. Her left hand was bunched in the folds of her cardigan. Her mouth was open as she gulped at the air. 'Go to your class,' MacLasher told her, 'and explain why you're late.' He turned to the boys and continued with the orgy of terror.

The path to school led round a football pitch and ended at a crossroads. A left turn led directly to the school gates, just a hundred yards away while the road to the right offered the forbidden freedom of the seashore with its promise of adventure. Shortly after my confrontation with MacLasher as a slothful miscreant, I came one morning to the crossroads. It was one of those early spring days when, as a twelve-year old boy, I felt that irrepressible surge of new life blowing in the kindly west wind. Less than a mile away the spring tide would be ebbing away from the foreshore, leaving crystal clear rock pools exposed to the sunlight with their hidden treasures of multi-coloured seaweed and dark rocks, hiding places for green crabs or perhaps a stranded flounder.

Chapter Two

It was to be a morning of double maths in a classroom with no windows to the world outside and therefore very limited opportunity to indulge in daydreaming. As I poised, undecided in the saddle, one foot on the ground, I saw the bus which brought pupils from surrounding villages leaving the school gates and reasoned that by the time I put my cycle away in the bike shed I would almost certainly be late for assembly, giving MacLasher the perfect opportunity to flog me. Repeat offenders were treated with particular ferocity; often, it was said, suffering six paralysing lashes to each hand. I crossed the road, turned right and headed for the beach.

It would be impossible for me to exaggerate the soaring sense of elation and freedom which thrilled through me as I left behind the prospect of ninety minutes of maths under the sullen tutelage of MacLasher. I stood up out of my bicycle saddle and powered the pedals furiously until the wind whistled through my hair. As I approached the seashore I called out to the seagulls as they floated on the thermals before wheeling and flying again upwind towards me, to turn once more and sweep away and away, unfettered and free, silvery white in the bright spring sky. It was all too much for me; my heart was too full. A large number of oyster catchers were picking their way through the shimmering sand, immaculate in their black and white plumage, set off perfectly by glowing red legs, and bills with which they probed for tiny molluscs and sand worms as they followed the ebb of the tide. I laid down my bike and walked among the rock pools.

The foreshore was quite deserted but far out to sea was a boat; fishermen, perhaps, but they couldn't see me. This day was all mine, I told myself, but I wondered why my eyes had misted over, and why they were filling with tears, until I was forced to blink and the salty drops spilled down my cheeks. It wasn't that I was unhappy, far from it. It was simply that it was all too much for me. At that moment I cared nothing at all for the consequences of my truancy, nor did I dream that those glorious future days of profligate irresponsibility would exact a cost which I would be required to pay for many feckless years, as the carefree attitude which was to become an addiction would lead me down many an enticing pathway in search of that elusive sense of liberty, only to discover that true freedom remains a tantalising illusion which is beyond reach of natural humankind. As Solomon noted in chapter 14 verse 12 of his collection of proverbs (NIV), 'There is a way that appears to be right, but in the end, it leads to death.' But I was determined that this would not be the last time that I would share my forbidden adventure with the sky and the birds, the sea and the wind, and if I were to repeat this thrilling defiance of draconian authority, it would be necessary to devise a scheme to evade detection.

There were six in our immediate family, but twenty or more other children shared the mansion which was our home. It had been acquired by an international missionary society as a temporary home for the children of those who had been called to various countries, many of them remote, inhospitable and considered unsuitable for the safe nurture, care and education of their children. These missionaries had taken the agonising decision to leave their children in the care of my parents, who themselves had served in the Congo, and who had committed themselves to the upkeep of the home and the welfare of the children.

The home used notepaper especially printed with its official logo and it was a simple matter for me to sneak unnoticed into the office and take a little sheaf of notepaper which would be used to forge excuses for absence. 'John has been suffering from chronic stomach pains,' I would write. It seemed sensible to me to target my ailments at a specific anatomical area in order to suggest a genuine ongoing affliction rather than offer a confusing plethora of symptoms which may well be deemed to be contrived. For several months my absences were excused, endorsed by the official looking notes which I would present on my return to school, sometimes after three days of absence. In the rush and bustle of a home of twenty-five or thirty children it was not difficult to blend in with the rest. I simply had to be home for lunch time and for tea at four thirty. There were only one or two classes which I shared with my brother and I was careful to attend them.

During those days I spent hours exploring the magnificent sandstone cliffs and caves of the north east coast. There were places where I was hidden, even from the seagulls, which would follow after me, diving and screaming aggressively around my head if I was too near their nesting sites; I would climb down into Dickmont Den, then scramble up the rocks to the entrance to the cave, twenty feet up in the cliff face. A rush of enervating energy would meet me as I clambered down into the heart of the cave which opens at its far end to the sea. I would stand on the mass of glistening rock as a dark wave bulged up the narrowing channel as if to engulf me, before sinking away as though in exhaustion, before being gathered up in the renewed energy of the wave which followed after. They would strain and swell together, confined to the deep gully at my feet as though warning me to stand clear. The thrill of those moments was intoxicating as I crept, as near as I dared, to the threatening power of the waves which had set out for this very place from far out in the North Sea. The wind which had stirred them into life and urged them on roared through the cave, tugging at my clothes as, restrained by a timeless rhythm, the surges of power rose and fell like a mighty, cosmic heartbeat.

I would spare a thought for my hapless classmates, languishing in the close confinement of MacLasher's classroom with its confusing mass of algebraic equations scrawled across the dusty blackboard. He would be crouched at his desk, ears pricked to catch the slightest hint of illicit communication; a select few of his intellectually gifted victims would be scratching away at their jotting books, while others sat with the vacant look of closely confined battery chickens. Now and then MacLasher would leave his desk. Anyone who had been doodling on the back page of their jotter was now in deadly peril. The challenge was to turn, unseen, to the page where a futile effort had been made to solve the day's mathematical proposition without being spotted. It was of little interest to MacLasher whether the day's work page showed any real understanding of the task set out on the blackboard.

Among my favourite haunts was Kelly Den, with its long disused railway line, decorated with little clusters of wild flowers, its castle with a garden rich with sumptuous rhododendrons, the lake behind the big house where brown trout would dart away in all directions like fleeting shadows and hide under the floating weed banks of the burn which ran down to the sea, and the fallen tree which made a bridge over the stream.

Then there was 'Freek' dam, fed by the River Lunan, with its legendary monster trout whose name was Auld Tam. He was a wily specimen who treated all efforts to catch him with dignified disdain. One warm afternoon I saw him, all three and a half pounds of him, like an elegant, speckled vision floating in a dream. I had heard tales of Auld Tam, told in reverent tones by those who claimed to have seen him. Fly, worm or minnow, it was said, would never take him; he would ignore them all. I watched him that magical day, languidly cruising confidently along a clear channel very near the bank of the dam, as though he could sense my ghastly primeval longing to hook him, net him and whack him to death. His golden eye watched me contemptuously as I walked slowly alongside him. Barely moving his tail, with the slightest flick he smoothly circumnavigated the writhing lobworm which I had cast perfectly just ahead of him. To my shame, after several futile attempts to lure him to an ignoble fate, frustration persuaded me to try to foul hook him and I cast a large treble hook across him. As though acutely aware of this real new danger, he thwarted my cowardly efforts to take him by diving and turning in a blinding flash and disappearing into the weed. I never saw him again.

Chapter Three

Inevitably, the repetitive production of the same old excuse for my frequent absences began to lose authenticity. I overheard hints that my parents should be contacted, a prospect which filled me with real dread. The theme of a gastric disorder, however, had served me well and I decided to try it directly on my mother. On a day when the prospect of a double history lesson under the excruciatingly boring supervision of a teacher we called Droopy, I refused breakfast and presented myself as suffering from the old chestnut which was, of course, chronic stomach pain.

There followed two or three months of sanctioned absences. It was true that I wasn't free to roam the backroads of Angus, but school had become anathema to me, and reading books in my own room was infinitely preferable to listening to the lifeless monotone of dismal Droopy draining the last vestige of interest from various historical events or watching a red admiral butterfly shredding its wings against the classroom window of a French lesson in a heart-breaking attempt to escape to the airy freedom of the summer morning.

Doctor Christie was a tall, strong and personable man. His deep, echoing voice was edged with a gravelly tone which bore testimony to his addiction to nicotine. He wore elegant three-piece tweed suits which smelled strongly of tobacco which I found sinfully exciting. His hair was black and wavy with a centre parting and besides a moustache, he had a permanent five o'clock shadow. Mother had called him for the second or third time in the hope that yet another examination would provide a diagnosis for my affliction.

I had been referred to the local hospital as an outpatient and had suffered the discomfort and indignity of several enemas which had inevitably resulted in copious discharges of soapy water, accompanied by outrageous bubbling, very noisy emissions of air, but little else. But by far the most disappointing aspect of those embarrassing medical procedures was the mandatory baring of my bottom in the face of Rosemary, the prettiest nurse you ever saw. She had the softest gentlest little hands and a voice which would soothe a raging fever. Any fantasies I had entertained when I first set eyes on her jet-black wavy hair and pale blue eyes were rudely shattered. I was required to lie facing the wall in the foetal position as she donned a pair of gloves and applied the necessary lubrication in preparation for the insertion of the intrusive rubber tubing. The prospect of standing hand in hand with her, looking out to sea on a moonlit night as the sea birds slept on the gently rising waves faded rapidly as she pumped me up until I felt I would burst.

Doctor Christie's final examination on the fatal day ended with the doctor and my mother speaking in hushed, conspiratorial voices, leaving me feeling rather uneasy. Had the good doctor actually discovered some serious ailment after all? It would serve the cause of justice if I was genuinely ill, after all the deceit and flagrant lies with which I had worried my dear mother simply to avoid the disciplined conformity of formal education.

Mother said goodbye to Doctor Christie. She called me into the office. 'I need to talk with you, John,' she said gravely. 'It's come to this. You're suffering from grumbling appendicitis. You're going to hospital for an operation.' This was madness surely! Nothing short of a travesty of medical ethics! It was time to make a miraculous recovery! I had gone too far and been too convincing, wincing with feigned discomfort as the doctor had kneaded my stomach. 'Tender there?' he would enquire as he carefully explored yet again with gently probing fingers the same spot, and I would nod weakly, trying to look as though I was a brave, but suffering patient. How could I have known that the very abdominal area which had consistently caused a fake twinge of pain as the good doctor pressed the lower right side of my tummy was the exact location of my appendix?

'I really do feel so much better,' I told mother. 'Couldn't we just leave it for now, or at least go for a second opinion?' One of the oft quoted Bible verses in my father's extensive collection of salutary scriptures sounded in my head with remorseless insistence: 'Be sure your sin will find you out!'

There was to be no reprieve. Poor mother had had enough. Shortly after my thirteenth birthday I was admitted to the local infirmary where my perfectly healthy appendix was needlessly removed. In those days a relatively minor operation such as an appendectomy would leave the patient with a wound at least five inches long and hospitalisation was to be expected for a week or more. In addition, it was thought that at least a further week should be allowed for the wound to heal properly and no strenuous activity should be undertaken. Mother, however, could never bear to see me, or anyone else, unoccupied and one day she seized upon the perfect opportunity for the useful employment of my time.

Chapter Four

My little sister Lizzie was now eight or nine months old, and mother had the inexplicable notion that I should take her out in her pram for a walk. No objections of mine, however insistent, could bring about a change of mind. The pram was one of those old coach-built conveyances, heavy and elaborately sprung. I pointed out that my wound had not completely healed, that the weather was bitterly cold and that the received medical advice was rest without physical strain. I was put to shame at once as she regaled me with a familiar account of her early work in Africa. Despite suffering from a strained heart, she had often trekked through the dense Ituri forest to bring the gospel news to remote villages. I was left with an image of her, resplendent in a pith helmet and white cotton, hacking her way through the bush alongside a fellow missionary. In those days, she told me, lions and leopards roamed the bush, and here was I, a sturdy thirteen-year old, refusing to take my precious baby sister for an afternoon stroll. She ended her admonition with one of her very favourite sayings. 'Come on, lad,' she urged, 'Satan finds mischief for idle hands to do!'

Both our parents made such an extravagant fuss over Lizzie that I began to secretly dislike her. It seemed as though their entire world was wrapped up in their 'miracle' baby. Mother always paid her the honour of referring to her by her full title. It was 'Elizabeth Anne' this, or 'Elizabeth Anne' that, as if she was third in line to the throne of the United Kingdom and the

Commonwealth. No indulgence was too extreme concerning Elizabeth Anne and mother simply delighted in dressing her up like a cherished dolly, with colour co-ordinated baby clothes of the finest quality. On the day of our outing mother had settled on a pink outfit, which included a fetching little bonnet held in place by a pink satin ribbon; then there was the pink dress, and a soft warm cardigan of pink brushed wool. The ensemble was set off by a pink pillow trimmed with a pink frill and the snug pink blanket lay beneath a pink coverlet filled with down and trimmed with pink lace.

As I set off down the tree-lined drive with the pram and its peacefully sleeping occupant, I reasoned that my present embarrassing situation was all the fault of MacLasher. Had he not been on guard at the school door on that day of my first truancy, my life would doubtless have taken quite a different turn. Had I not tasted the intoxicating freedom of that first glorious morning exploring the seashore, I would not have become a habitual truant, cursed with a pathological hatred of disciplined confinement. The issue was perfectly clear. I could trace the responsibility for all my serious misdeeds unerringly back to MacLasher. My truancy, my deceitfulness, the bitter shame of my enforced, disgusting exposure to the angelic nurse Rosemary, my shameless hoodwinking of the noble Doctor Christie, the consequent removal of my appendix, to say nothing of the deep concern of my mother, all were directly attributable to MacLasher, who, I reasoned, certainly had a great deal to answer for.

The road I had taken passed by a prefabricated estate. It was a danger zone, simply because a number of my school mates lived there. Some, like Billy, were pretty tough. His father was a wrestler and had taught Billy several secret throws and agonising holds which gave him an unfair advantage in a brawl and which he liked to practise on people in the playground. It was wise to avoid Billy, and you certainly didn't want to be seen by him pushing a pram with a baby who looked exactly like an overdressed sleeping dolly. It was with some relief that I passed the last of the prefabs without being noticed.

Chapter Five

I was making for Hercules Den, a secluded walk which was just on the western edge of town. Turn off the main road, and immediately you were hidden from sight. The way through the den led past bare trees and ragged undergrowth, and autumn leaves which had fallen on the muddy path made progress hazardous. In spite of the lurching and bumping of her conveyance, Lizzie slept peacefully on, although the immaculate white pram tyres were now shod with sticky mud and wet leaves. Twenty feet or so below the footpath, the Brothock Burn flowed seductively over green tinged pebbles, swirling round small rocks and then, caught in lively eddies, tiny whirlpools continuously formed, to flow away and away forever, drawn by ancient currents to the North Sea.

I stood still for some time gazing in fascination at the burn. The winter rains had added life and energy to the dark green water weed which streamed like flowing hair over patches of clean gravel. All at once a small trout ventured out of its hiding place in the weeds, followed by a second. Within a minute three or four more had joined the little shoal, along with a fish that must have been almost a quarter of a pound, a veritable monster for this stretch of water! He took his favoured position behind the largest rock and hovered, his pectoral fins flickering, holding him in perfect poise, ready for an instant move should danger threaten, or the current bring some edible morsel within striking distance.

Over the past seventy years, I have often wondered exactly why I was all at once possessed of an inexplicable urge to be close to the burn with its rippling life. Perhaps it was the water vole which had appeared from a burrow on the far bank, only to dart back to safety when it saw me. I have no answer or explanation for my compelling urge to clamber down to the water's edge and somehow be in touch with the promise of an exciting, unknown future life. Quite possibly I was in need of psychiatric attention, but in those far off days such problems among young folk were not thought to be worthy of serious consideration.

I found a place which seemed to offer a very steep but accessible route of descent down to the water's edge and gingerly set off with poor Lizzie ahead of me, or rather below me as I bent over, clinging to the pram which hung perilously, front wheels out in the air, as though feeling for a firm footing. It was one of those times when you almost instantly regret what you are doing and actually attempt to talk sense to yourself. Yet, inexplicably it seems, there is no going back.

I was ten or twelve feet above the water's edge when I dramatically lost my footing. I sat down heavily and lost my hold of Lizzie, who, until this exact moment had remained blissfully asleep. As though in slow motion, the pram leapt downwards and outwards like a petulant horse which has escaped the restrictions of its halter. After only one spectacular bounce the front wheels totally failed to negotiate a large stone and catapulted by its powerful springs the wretched vehicle, along with Lizzie, still pristine in all her finery, somersaulted and came to rest upside down in the mud at the burn side. The frilly coverlet and the matching pillow had floated away together on impact and were trapped at the edge of the stream like a stricken, ridiculously pink swan with its dying cygnet. The pram wheels were spinning like those of a wrecked motor car which has been involved in a fatal accident.

Notwithstanding my recent surgical wound, I seized the front wheels and turned the heavy pram over leaving Lizzie, who was unmoving, trapped beneath the mattress and an under blanket. Caring nothing for mud or water, I threw all paraphernalia aside and lifted the earth's most treasured and pampered baby out of the mire. Thankfully, I quickly discovered why she had remained so quiet so far. She had been quite unable to scream, simply because her face was immersed in muddy water, which, as she opened her mouth, dribbled copiously down her chin.

It was some time before she had gulped sufficient air to deliver a scream loud enough, commensurate with her assessment of her situation, but when she finally filled her lungs the resulting wail was truly terrifying. The passage of time has not dulled my vivid memory of the inside of Lizzie's wide-open mouth, which was so remarkable simply because it was the only clean, unsullied part of her entire person. I watched with fascination, the whole picture framed in mud, as the pink cavern containing what I perceived to be her vibrating tonsils, bawled unintelligible accusations into my face.

I laid Lizzie at the verge of the burn, recovered the lost pillow and the sodden cover from downstream and tried my best to pull myself together. The constant distraction of my poor little sister's wailing as she lay wet through and obviously distressed made it difficult to concentrate. I gathered the soiled accoutrements together and piled them into the pram. I would have to drag the wretched thing, climbing backwards up to the path. By the time I returned for Lizzie, she was too exhausted to cry any more. I made a futile effort to wipe her face with the sodden coverlet, which left her looking as though some incompetent make-up artist had gone to work on her and left her looking exactly like a grimy ship's engineer in one of those British black and white disaster movies.

I hurried home and limped up the long tree lined drive, crouching awkwardly over the pram, trying my best to convey the impression of a pitiable youth wrestling manfully with the agony of a severely compromised surgical wound. Mother, who had been anxiously looking out of a window for the return of her pampered princess, appeared from the front porch and strode out to meet us. Anyone who ever saw our mother 'on the warpath,' as we called it, would understand why I prayed a desperate prayer for protection from the wrath to come.

While there remained ten yards between us, I decided that I must make a strong case in mitigation before the full implications of Lizzie's perilous outing could be grasped. Holding onto the pram with one hand, I bent over and shuddered with imaginary pain. 'It was my wound,' I said tremulously with what I judged might just be the right blend of pathos and accusation. My purpose was to appeal to both her maternal instinct, and at the same time tactfully to remind her of her stubborn insistence that I should be forced into such an ill-advised duty. But any hope that mother's concern for me and my implied critical condition might take precedence over her concern for her infinitely precious baby was a gross error of judgement.

She reached out and seized Lizzie as though snatching her from a blazing fire. She held her tight against her breast, not caring for the muddy water which she inadvertently squeezed from Lizzies soiled clothing. "You naughty boy!" she kept saying with an increasing emphasis on the word 'naughty'. Like an opera singer's repetitive practice session, as she strives again and again for yet more intensity at the top of her range, mother seemed caught up in the spirit of an urgent warning to the world. 'Naughty! Naughty! Naughty boy! What have you done! What have you done! Naughty! Naughty! NAUGHTY boy!'

I could see it was no use trying to reason with her, yet I had no choice except to stick to my guns. 'It wasn't my fault! I was enjoying a nice walk through Hercules Den and suddenly I had a terrific spasm of pain in my wound. I tried my best to hold on to Lizzie, but I lost control and the pram just ran away with itself and turned over and tipped Lizzie out at the edge of the burn. I had a struggle to rescue her and sort it all out, but I managed to bring her safely home, even though my wound...'

I wasn't permitted to finish my plea of mitigation. Mother had turned and set off for the house, leaving me to drag the mud-spattered pram with its soiled contents up to the porch. She stopped and turned to look straight at me. 'Wound? Wound?' she said, 'I'll give you a wound, my lad, a wound you'll never forget!' But her threat never materialised. It was made in the heat of the moment and she was overwrought. The happy truth is that, given the mitigating circumstances, my punishment didn't really fit my crime: I was never permitted to take Lizzie out in her pram again.

Epilogue

In all this world, there never was a mother like ours. She was to pray for me tirelessly for thirty-five more years, during which the continuing enticement of feckless irresponsibility, self-indulgence and self-justification left me stranded without hope or a future. In my forty-seventh year, mother's prayers for me were answered, and God himself arranged the circumstances and the encounters which brought me face to face with Jesus. I committed my life to him and was called to pastor a village Baptist church where I served for eleven years, followed by twenty years of humanitarian and missionary work in Africa.

But that's another story.

Love, Joy, Peace

Introduction

The Coast Mission was a gospel hall just a stone's throw from the shore of the North Sea in the area known in Arbroath as 'the fit o' the toon.' A Sunday evening visit to the little mission was considered by us children to be a weekly treat. We lived in a missionaries' children's home in a mansion on the western side of town and each week we would set off for the 'Coastie'—as we called it—to attend the evening service. The journey which led us through town to the safety of the Mission took us past the Picture House, where a queue of condemned sinners was waiting for the doors to open so that they may be swallowed up into a dark world of unmitigated evil devised and controlled by the Devil and his angels. Like John Bunyan's pilgrim who manfully resisted the tantalising delights of Vanity Fair we would glance at the lurid posters which festooned the entrance to the cinema and inwardly quiver with that fatal curiosity which leads the unwary to pass through the door that leads to destruction.

One of the highlights of our evening out, however, was the inevitable interruption of our pilgrimage through the town as we reached the shop window of Tom Clark's sports and fishing tackle shop, where we would fall foul of that most subtle boyhood temptation of covetousness. Abandoning ourselves to the lusts of the flesh we would embark upon a shameless orgy of 'bagsing' as many of the delights which adorned the shop window as we possibly could. It was important that you safely bagged the particular object of your desire before securing as many lesser items as possible.

'I bags that Dawes lightweight racer,' Paul would say, and that was it. The racer was gone, having been properly and legally bagged. There could be no change of ownership, no swapping, no 'backie backs!'

'Yes, and I bags that Milbro spinning rod and reel.' That was Philip's dream because his fishing reel was a wooden cotton bobbin with a nail carefully tapped halfway home as a handle.

For me it was the 177 Diana air rifle. Seventy-five years have passed since those days when I would 'bags' that airgun on the way to the Coast Mission, but I can still clearly see in my mind's eye the large oblong ticket which hung from the trigger guard with its black and white drawing of an alluring wild looking woman with unruly flowing hair. Diana, goddess of the hunt! Mr Clark had written the price of the gun along the bottom of the ticket. £1.7.6, it said. I spent many blissful moments during that drifting, hazy hour before sleep bore me away, dreaming of Diana the huntress leading the way through imaginary forests and grasslands in search of prey as I followed with the air rifle which bore her name.

Once our favoured objects had been safely 'bagged', we would ransack the window display until nothing was left. Interest gradually waned as we worked our way through the stock. A heavy Hercules bicycle with a chain guard and rod brakes, fishing waders, climbing boots and heavy woollen socks, a sheath knife, a fly-tying vice, bait boxes, a folding stool. Most of the more mundane items were regarded as boobies and were only claimed out of a sense of duty to the competitive spirit of covetousness which had ensnared us, but despite fading enthusiasm we did not spare a single item and continued on our pilgrimage to the Coast Mission, perfectly satisfied with our frantic spell of window shopping.

Chapter One

Mr Maxwell was a kindly soul. He presided over the mission, aided by his sons, Tom and Walter. Tom was a good looking, engaging young man with a fluid, easy manner; he was the mission soloist and had developed a lilting, crooning style of singing which my father considered to be rather worldly. He would have preferred a more straightforward delivery and less of a performance. Tom would caress each word as though he might be singing to a particular member of the little congregation, and I suspect that our sister, Lily who was stunningly beautiful, may have fancied that she was the inspiration for Tom's yearning solos.

Tom's brother, Walter, was the preacher. By all accounts he was a gifted speaker, but to my shame I don't remember the actual content of any of his gospel messages. He seemed rather less easy-going than his brother and his delivery was earnest and compelling. There was an authority about Walter which was rooted in his sincere faith and even in those wanton and naive boyhood days I knew that he deserved to be taken seriously.

Each of Walter's messages ended with what was known as an 'appeal'. This practice seemed to be accepted as a mandatory feature of evangelical preaching. There is an inherent challenge in the gospel message which demands a response, positive or negative. A 'yes' or a 'no.' The alternative simply will not do and will leave the hearer high and dry, lost in no man's land. This non-committal attitude was famously adopted by Pontius Pilate who called for water and symbolically washed his hands in a vain attempt to absolve himself of any responsibility for the condemnation of Christ. Each time the gospel is presented in Spirit and truth an opportunity is offered to those who are present to respond. That is the essence of the message, so powerfully demonstrated through the preaching of the Apostle Peter, on that historic day recorded in Acts chapter 2, when the gospel was publicly proclaimed for the first time and the church was born.

Walter's appeals were characterised by such an earnest sincerity that I would feel genuinely sorry for him if there was no response. It was never intended to be easy, of course. A public commitment to repentance obviously implied that anyone answering the altar call, as the procedure was known, was someone with a number of guilty secrets, leaving the rest of the congregation with an irresistible temptation for morbid speculation. A convicted sinner would be required, in front of the whole assembly, to leave their seat, walk to the front and enter the door alone into the little side room, where a counsellor would presently join them, read a relevant verse or passage and teach them a simple prayer of commitment.

Taken seriously, this can certainly be a truly life changing miracle which remains a great mystery, but which, for forty years, eluded all my efforts personally to grasp and experience the wonder of the miracle.

'Is there one,' Walter would say, 'Is there one here tonight who would be free of the burden of their sin? Now, as every eye is closed and every head bowed, is there one?' Squinting out of the corner of one eye, I would watch the hunched shoulders and bowed heads of the congregation around me and wonder if they were all secretly tormented by their personal shortcomings. 'Every eye closed, and every head bowed.' Walter would remind us firmly, 'Is there one?' Had he noticed me peeking, I would wonder. As the minutes ticked by the atmosphere in the little gospel hall seemed almost unbearably tense. During the silences which Walter was careful to observe in order to build the pressure, you could hear the old wall clock inexorably claiming each passing second. Every time the clock ticks, it was said, a soul passes from this life into eternity.

'Is there one, brother, sister, aunt or uncle?' There was no escape, it seemed, but Walter would finally be obliged to give in and eventually he would pray a short prayer with special reference to those who may have resisted the call to respond to the message of the gospel. To the relief of some and the disappointment of others, the last hymn would be announced. I remember that a baleful song called 'Almost persuaded' seemed to feature frequently on these occasions, but no sooner had the last funereal notes faded away with the solemn words, 'Almost, but lost!' than the atmosphere would return to normal, with little or no reference to the message and much banal banter, as though the congregation was grateful to be relieved of the tension which had held them in thrall for the past ten minutes. It would not be uncommon to hear the latest news of someone's allotment and the danger of a late frost threatening their early potatoes.

Chapter Two

During the holiday season known as the 'Glasgow Fair Fortnight,' the town was bursting at the seams with visitors and as we made our way home up Arbroath High Street; our sister Lily always attracted the attention of a number of young men who were out on the prowl hoping to meet a young lady with the hope of friendship, fun and a holiday romance!

Perhaps I should pause for a few moments here and recount a true story which might help to illustrate the beguiling effect which our elder sister's looks seemed to have on the opposite sex. One Saturday afternoon she kindly offered to share a bag of chips with me. We chose Carini's fish and chip shop in Cairnie street, where just a couple of customers were waiting to be served. The shop was managed by an Italian lady assisted by her son who was about twenty years old. Above the fryers was a long mirror so that customers could be seen and served without coming face to face with the proprietor until it was time to pay. As we entered the shop, the young man had just lifted a large basketful of chips and was about to deposit them on the hot tray above the fryer, when he caught sight of Lily in the mirror. He stood spellbound, the basket of chips in his hand, as though transfixed. His mother spoke sharply to him in Italian and I can only assume that she said something like, 'Get on with it! What's the matter with you!' He didn't answer, but simply nodded towards the mirror image of our sister. 'Ah,' sighed the Mama, 'Belissimo! Belissimo!'

I remember Lily being quite polite when she was accosted with an offer of romantic companionship.

'Hello, darlin', I've been lookin' for you! Whaur've ye been a' ma' life! Dae ye fancy goin' somewhere nice?'

Lily slowed down, looked at her suitor and said, 'I'm sorry, I've already been somewhere nice this evening. I'm going home now.'

Encouraged and surprised by a response from such a delectable creature, the youth seemed confused and almost lost for words. A friend joined him, leaning over his shoulder to stare at our sister and within a few moments other young men gathered round until Lily was surrounded by a small crowd of eager swains. Her original suitor saw that he was in danger of losing the initiative to the opposition and attempted to press home his advantage.

'So, ye've been somewhere nice,' he said. 'Whaur wis that, the Picter Hoose?'

Lily shook her head dismissively as though appalled at the suggestion. 'I don't go to the pictures,' she said witheringly. 'Film stars live godless lives and the films they make are disgustingly sinful. No, I've been to the Coast Mission to hear the gospel!' Her little congregation, which had swelled as the minutes passed, seemed truly awestruck.

'The gospel, ye say, whit's that?'

Lily looked around at her audience and boldly proclaimed the apostolic doctrine of sin, righteousness and the certainty of judgement to come, and then emphasised the mercy and kindness of God who had sent his only Son into the world to give his life on a cross, carrying the burden of all the sin of this world in our place so that all who believe in him would be forgiven and given not only a new life and a fresh start, but a wonderful home in heaven. She ended by quoting John chapter 3 verse 16. So passionate and earnest was her presentation of the gospel that it was followed by a bewildered silence, which was broken at last by an angry voice.

'So why's a lovely lassie like you wastin' her time talkin' a load o' blethers!' It was the signal for a serious division of opinion.

'You just shut yer mooth!' said an indignant supporter loudly, 'it's nae blethers!' Turning to Lily he said, 'D'ye hae ony mair o' they stories?'

She explained that we must be home by eight o'clock, promised that we'd see them the following Sunday evening at the Coast

Mission at six o'clock sharp, and we all hurried home. I was so proud of our elder sister's witness, and although I suspect that her open air congregation, having consisted exclusively of teenage males, was enthralled more by Lily's natural magnetism and loveliness than her earnest presentation of the gospel. After many years, I have come to understand rather more of the power of the Holy Spirit to awaken a seed sown in the human heart, a seed which may have lain dormant for many years. Only the Good Shepherd knows if any eager young listener truly heard his voice that summer evening in Arbroath High Street.

Chapter Three

My twin brother, David was well on his way to a life of devoted Christian ministry. He was muscular and powerfully built and, apart from the odd occasion when he was provoked at school and broke a nose or two, he was a boy of outstanding virtue who never really appeared to be plagued by the demons which so effectively beguiled me. His exemplary obedience and godly use of his time contrasted sharply with my deceitful behaviour. I was ever on the lookout for discarded cigarette ends in the gutter which I would smoke in the nearest gents' toilets, not because I enjoyed the experience, but because it was such a disgraceful sin.

Each morning before school we would recite the day's verse. Mother would stand holding a large tin of sweets and a word-perfect rendering of the verse was rewarded by a dip into the treasure chest of brightly wrapped delights where one sweet may be selected and noisily enjoyed. I had developed the technique of palming one sweet while making an elaborate show of rummaging for another. The day came when I was discovered and disgraced, mother demanding that I open my hand and reveal the evidence of the sinfulness of my flesh, but I thought the punishment which was inflicted on me was quite petty. For a whole week I was required to learn and recite my daily verses without any reward.

As my tally of misdeeds mounted, my brother's righteousness was highlighted by the inevitable comparison with my waywardness. Each of my misdemeanours would be repeated by him in a voice which was pregnant with appalled virtue as though his soul was horribly offended by my very existence.

'You did what?' he would gasp, his eyes raised heavenwards, his whole demeanour exactly like one of those images of ancient saints which you sometimes see on stained glass windows. Before he was able to actually remind me of the sad details of my latest offence, he would make a 'Tut, tut' sound, which he would repeat at least ten times. 'You did what?' he would say again, 'You actually sneaked off and hid when you were supposed to be on dinner dishes! Mother says you just climbed a tree, heaved yourself over the wall and ran off.' It was time to bury his face in his hands, shake his head very slowly and launch into another despairing chorus of 'Tut, tut, tut!'

One day, following yet another lost battle with temptation, my twin, who I believe was truly concerned for my soul's eternal welfare, told me that he knew a secret which mother had whispered into his ear concerning my godless behaviour.

'It's because you're not a Christian,' he told me solemnly. 'Mother says that if you were a Christian you wouldn't do all those grievous things which so upset everyone. If you gave your heart to Jesus, you'd be a changed person.'

Strangely enough, I had never given this matter any thought. The very notion that Walter may have been appealing directly to me had never entered my head. However, since I had heard, over the years, several personal accounts of the conversion experience from various Christians I reckoned that I had little to lose.

Almost without fail there were certain beneficial elements in these accounts. More often than not the testimony would begin with a confession of previous shameful behaviour with varying degrees of greed, deceit and selfishness, all of which had left the testifier feeling unfulfilled and miserable with an empty vacuum in their lives. This condition seemed to apply to me with uncanny accuracy—what with my futile longing for the Diana air rifle. However, the three words which were almost inevitably used to describe the dramatic life changing transformation which had followed repentance and commitment were peace, joy and satisfaction, usually presented in that order. Weighed against the embarrassment of publicly exposing myself as a sneaky little sinner, it seemed that not only would I be set free from my frustrating obsession with the air rifle and be flooded with peace, joy and satisfaction, I would also be accepted as a real member of the family instead of the subject of whispered conversations, accompanied by pained expressions of holy shock as my latest misdeeds were trotted out to the accompaniment of many a beseeching heavenward glance.

Chapter Four

And so my mind was made up. The following Sunday evening, the Arbroath Coast Mission would be the scene of a conversion. I remember nothing of the readings or hymns or Walter's message that night. It all seemed quite irrelevant. All that mattered was the appeal, which I reckoned was sure to come. I wasted no time. As soon as Walter began to say, 'Perhaps there's someone here this evening…' I was up on my feet, making for the door of the side room. Once inside, I sat on a wooden bench looking at the bare floorboards which were worn and grey. Presently Mr Maxwell came in and quietly closed the door. I don't remember what he said but I can recall that his voice trembled with what seemed to be kindness. He read something from the New Testament which I probably knew by heart and then he asked me to repeat a prayer of repentance and commitment. After the 'amen' I waited expectantly for my whole being to be flooded with peace, joy and satisfaction but I was distracted by the sound of raised voices coming through the door. I didn't want to go out to face the congregation because I didn't think things had worked out properly. I had expected to feel different; peaceful and joyful and satisfied all at once but I felt none of those things, only a sense of disappointment and failure.

Our sister Lily gave me a hug and I had a struggle to keep myself from crying. No-one said anything but they were looking at me as if they were waiting for me to speak. As we all walked home the others were chattering away as though everything was quite normal, but I remained silent. There was nothing to say. That night our mother came quietly into our bedroom. She sat on my bed and stroked my hair. She had exactly the right sort of hands for this because they were so strong and gentle, and I could tell that she loved me and that she was pleased. She said that she was proud of me, and that God had laid his hand on me and that he had work for me to do. I daren't tell her that things didn't feel right because she was so pleased, but I sometimes wonder if God truly did accept me that evening in spite of the awful way in which I subsequently conducted my life. He is the only One who knows.

Epilogue

During the following thirty-seven years I would strive to reach out to Jesus in repentance on at least four occasions in various circumstances only to fall away as that elusive dream of peace, joy and satisfaction failed to materialise. Perhaps these were stepping-stones on a dangerous journey across raging waters until, at the age of forty-seven I was at last brought by God's grace and kindness to that place of life transforming, surging joy which is the gift of the Holy Spirit to the genuinely repentant sinner. In my experience, I have found that this joy ebbs and flows but it remains a constant ineradicable source of power to the poor sinner whose eyes remain fixed on Christ the Redeemer.

'Now is your time of grief, but I will see you again, and you will rejoice,' said Jesus according to John 16 verse 22, 'And no-one will take away your joy.' (NIV)

Eleven years of ministry at a village Baptist church have been followed by eighteen years of evangelistic work in Africa along with the rescue, education and vocational training of thousands of orphans and desperately needy children.

Today, in my eighty-fourth year, I look back at that bare, simple little room in Arbroath Town Mission, and wonder at the kindness and undying love of God.

How Great Thou Art
Chapter One

I was possibly the most irritating Christian convert who ever saw the light. Perhaps my urge to save the world and everyone in it was due to so many years of stubborn resistance as the pressure of mother's prayers which built up deep within me, like an overwhelming body of water, burst at last through the crumbling walls of stubborn resistance. In retrospect, I am not surprised that some of the war-bitten, battle-weary Christians whom I met in those early days would make every effort to avoid me, as I would seize any opportunity to share my latest personal spiritual revelation.

From early childhood, along with our family, I had been required to learn a daily Bible verse. A successful repetition brought the entitlement of a dip into the community sweet tin. I should confess that I soon perfected the art of using my little finger to hook one sweet into the palm of my hand while choosing another which I would pick out carefully, using my forefinger and thumb. Despite this unholy deceitfulness, I inevitably committed many of the Psalms to memory, including the 176 verses of 119, besides some of the great prophetic passages from Isaiah and various 'key' verses from the epistles, including entire letters as well as The Sermon on the Mount.

In my late teens, I escaped into a world of illusory freedom, where I lived a profligate life and no ungodly practice was off limits, yet I could not entirely escape the powerful influence of my family's prayers. Mother would spend two weeks at a time, living in a small caravan in a remote Angus glen, where she would fast and pray for me, day after day and long into the night.

I vividly remember being involved in one of many marathon poker games which took place in a room with no natural light. In those days unlicensed poker games were illegal, and in certain towns the police might raid at any time, so windows were covered with heavy curtains or old blankets. After two or three days of intense concentration it was easy to lose track of time. It was as though that dismal room, clogged with tobacco smoke and the reek of unwashed bodies, was entirely separate from the world outside. While you were closed in there, nothing else existed. The poker game was all there was. And so how could it be that holed up in that foul place where I shared the company of those poor lost souls I should all at once feel a wave of overwhelming purity and love sweeping over me like a flood?

It was up to me to make a bet and the other players sat waiting for me to take my turn and move the game on.

'Up to you,' the dealer said, 'Call or pass.'

'Come on, come on!' snarled one of the players who was losing heavily, 'I'm doin' my money here! Call or pass, man!'

But I sat, staring at my cards, laid out on the table. All at once they meant nothing, nothing at all.

'What time is it? It's important. I need to know!' I demanded.

Looking at his watch, the agitated loser said impatiently, 'Four forty-five. It's a quarter to five. Why, whass a matter wid you?'

'But is it afternoon or morning?' I asked.

'It's Saturday morning!' he shouted angrily. 'Quarter to five on Saturday morning. Now just call or pass. Are you in or out?' I felt a painful longing rising in my heart.

'My mother's awake,' I said simply. 'I can't play anymore. She's praying for me. Deal me out.'

I threw my cards into the middle of the table and pocketed my money. An awkward silence descended momentarily on that room. Poor, tough, dyed-in-the-wool sinners averted their eyes as though mysteriously chastened. It was as if a great unseen hand had covered the place like a shadow and stilled those voices so often raised in crude blasphemy, including my own.

At the age of forty-seven, through an intricate and seemingly unrelated series of circumstances including chance encounters, moments of solitude when I would find myself repeating scriptures learned in childhood and, finally, the passing of an old gambler friend, God, my forever gracious Father, called me to himself. I wholeheartedly repented of my unspeakable sins and surrendered my besmirched and pitiful life to the control of Christ. The Word, which I had been obliged to memorise daily for more than a decade, caught fire as the Holy Spirit breathed his promised understanding and life into those texts and passages which I had always considered to be nothing but rather fine literature. I would hurry to church on a Sunday morning and corner the nearest prospective victim.

'Listen to this,' I'd say eagerly. 'Here's what I read yesterday. You're just going to love this!' But why, I would wonder, is this fellow believer looking around so desperately, as though planning a way of escape.

'This is Hebrews chapter 2 verse 11,' I'd go on, determined to deliver my life-changing verse for the edification of my Christian brother who was looking just a bit peaky.

'Just listen to this now. Try and take this in. "Both the one who makes men holy and those who are made holy are of the same family. So Jesus is not ashamed to call them brothers."'

The thrilling grace expressed in this verse had so enraptured me the previous morning; I had leapt from my chair punching the air in excitement. Filled to overflowing with spiritual adrenalin, I simply had to escape the claustrophobia of our tiny sitting room. I rushed out into the morning, looking for a space which might contain my ardour; I ran helter-skelter down to the river, crossed the bridge on to Stourbridge common and ran across the grass waving both hands at the sky.

'Brother Jesus! Brother Jesus!' I called out, laughing. 'Can this be? Can this truly be?'

I thought of him, all I'd ever learned of him, from earliest childhood, his teaching, his compassion, his miracles and above all, his determined submission to the horrors of the cross. I thought of his loneliness, his abandonment, his humiliating rejection, his supreme authority over death as he willingly surrendered his life. I thought of the blazing energy of the Spirit of holiness by whose power he was declared to be the Son of God by his resurrection from the dead—Jesus Christ our Lord! And this Jesus is not ashamed to call me his brother!

Even now as I write this, thirty-six years later, my heart is full and my eyes are burning. It's not that I am especially holy, or worthy, quite the reverse. It's that God is infinitely gracious.

My poor captive audience of a single soul listened nervously to my verse. His discomfort was palpable. His eyes darted from side to side as he looked over each of my shoulders in turn, hoping for deliverance. All at once he saw a way of escape.

'S'cuse me,' he gasped, 'I've just noticed an old friend I haven't seen in months,' and he ducked away, clambering over the pews, knocking his shins painfully as he fled to the other side of the church. A week or two later, my Pastor advised me solemnly to calm down.

'The members are murmuring about you,' he said. 'They're saying you're a fanatic.' I thought for a second before answering:

'Do you think the Apostle Paul was a fanatic?' I asked.

Chapter Two

Most of my new Christian associates avoided me. Flaunting what I considered to be my prodigious Bible knowledge, I would dominate every conversation. My particular hobby horse concerned the church's prayer life. I couldn't understand why a thriving church with a Sunday morning attendance of three hundred souls or more could shrivel away to almost nothing when it was time to pray. I would harass and harry anyone whom I could engage in conversation. Standing up in the church's Business meeting, which was always enthusiastically attended, I made an impassioned plea for the members to join together in the weekly prayer gathering.

'Don't you believe that God actually wants to hear and answer our prayers? Don't you believe he's ready to listen and that he delights in our fellowship with him? Haven't you understood the immeasurable cost of that open door into his presence?'

I felt a wall of resentment, even antagonism against me. Who, or what, did I think I was! A convert of only a few weeks, still wet behind the ears! Why doesn't someone shut him up! Only the faithful little handful of regulars would turn up week by week, and we enjoyed some wonderful times of fellowship together. Some members said Tuesday evenings were inconvenient. So I asked for permission to open the church hall at 5 a.m. and announced that I would be there each day until 7.30 a.m. for prayer. I would be up and away at 4. 45 a.m., cycling across town, sometimes in pouring rain, singing at the top of my voice:

> *'And when I think that God, his son not sparing,*
> *sent him to die, I scarce can take it in...*
> *How great thou art...!'*

Sometimes a new convert would join me, and now and then a dear saintly old lady would arrive on her bicycle. But what really troubled me was that most of the congregation thought the early morning prayer meetings were a joke and frequently said so. It seemed that the only people who really listened were old acquaintances from my past life. Some would stand staring at me wistfully as I told the story of my conversion and the exciting new life which powered me out of bed each morning with a song in my heart. They would say things like,

'That's truly wonderful. I'm really happy for you. At least you've got something to live for. I wish something like that would happen to me. You must let me know how you get on!'

I was addicted to nicotine. Due to many years of living on my wits, cigarettes had become an essential part of my constitution and the sublime excitement of the realisation of God's grace, so kindly extended to me, had in no way diminished my need of what I would call a 'gasper' at least twenty times daily. We had been brought up with dire warnings of the spiritual dangers of smoking.

'Light a cigarette, and you will light the fire of hell inside you,' we were told, yet I had no qualms at all about the habit. Not that

I flaunted what I believed was my freedom to indulge this freedom in front of my parents or, indeed, other Christians, but I made no secret of it. I shared many a cigarette with a number of non-Christians whom the Lord graciously used me to bring to faith.

One of my most cynical critics was Stella, my long-suffering and loyal wife, at that time of almost thirty years. She has somehow managed to put up with me for more than sixty years to date and that has never been easy for her! She herself had inexplicably begun a patient and steady spiritual journey, attending a local Baptist church, much to my scorn and amusement. And now she simply didn't understand what had come over me.

We were the owners of a fairly successful antiques business and I had been an enthusiastic partner, willing to work from dawn to dusk, scouring auctions and renovating various treasures, but I had now, characteristically, lost interest, and I would spend my days visiting old acquaintances with the thrilling message of new life in Christ. From boyhood I had rebelled against discipline and a woeful lack of perseverance had always been my fatal drawback. Stella could see only too well that our business no longer interested me and was convinced that my enthusiasm for this sudden religious fervour was merely another passing fad.

'Look here,' she said one day, 'you need to make up your mind! Either you're a preacher, or evangelist or whatever, or we're in business. Tell you what, never mind about running around trying to convert your old friends, why don't you start with your neighbour? What about poor Cecily? Don't you think she needs some attention and spiritual encouragement?'

We had seen Cecily only once. It was on a summer afternoon when Freddie, her husband, with the help of a visitor had carried her down from her room and sat her in the garden. We had been outside, enjoying the sun when we first saw her. I had never seen anyone so cruelly disabled by extreme arthritis. Wracked and shrunk by years of pain, her diminutive body was so bent that her head was pressed against her breast so that she could see nothing but her bony and misshapen hands, fidgeting on her lap. Her tiny feet dangled three or four inches from the ground. To my shame, I shuddered with revulsion and immediately turned away and went inside.

During the following two days I sank into despair. All enthusiasm and joy leaked out of me like water from a rusty bucket. I could think only of Jesus who was never repelled by sickness or palsy or blindness or even the untouchable. A man with leprosy came to him and begged him on his knees, 'If you are willing, you can make me clean.' Filled with compassion, Jesus reached out his hand and touched the man.

''I am willing,' he said. 'Be clean!' Immediately the leprosy left him and he was cured.' (Mark 1:41-42, NIV)

Stella was right! I had been repelled by a gentle and needy soul whom Jesus cherished and loved. This was a lesson well remembered twenty-five years later in the service of Christ in Malawi, central Africa, where the Dawn Centre was founded, a home, shelter and school which continuously brings hope and a future to upwards of fifty seriously handicapped children.

One afternoon I rang the bell next door. 'Good afternoon, Freddie,' I said as Cecily's husband opened the door. He was a small, balding man with fussy hands which were always moving, as though they were looking for something to do. He took a kindly interest in our affairs and had listened to the story of my conversion with an approving look.

'Yes, yes, yes,' he had remarked. 'Yes, yes, you are on the right track. That's just what the world needs. We need the gospel. Not enough people like you and me around nowadays. Nobody cares. Who cares for the carers? No, no! Nobody cares.'

As he spoke his hands fluttered about and his head shook slowly as though deploring the world's lack of care for the carers, while asserting its need for the gospel, although when I asked if he had ever made a personal commitment to Christ he became flustered.

'It's the world, not me,' he said a little sternly as if I had completely misunderstood the purpose of what he called 'The Gospel'.

As I stood at his open door on that day, Freddie looked up at me inquiringly, with an optimistic expression. I began awkwardly, clearing my throat.

'Freddie,' I said, feeling that my face was flushed and hot, 'I've come to enquire about Cecily. What I mean is, do you think she'd like a visit? After all, we're neighbours, Freddie, and I haven't even had a chance to greet her.' He didn't seem a bit surprised.

'Oh yes,' he said without hesitation, 'Yes, yes, yes! This is most kind, most kind. Well, well, well, she will be pleased. Do, just go up. Second door on the left. She's watching T.V., but don't worry, you can switch it off. She won't mind. Indeed she'll be delighted. Go and introduce yourself and I'll put the kettle on. I'll bring up a tray with tea and biscuits.'

The house had a clean, polished smell. It was an imposing town house, but all the Victorian features which had characterised the interior had been ruthlessly removed and smoothed away in what Freddie was to assure me had been a project of modernisation. The bannisters and the balustrade had been boxed in with cream painted plywood and the stair treads were finished in non-slip vinyl, secured by reeded aluminium strips.

The purpose of this remorseless renovation, I was to learn, was the avoidance of dust. Carpets had been replaced with linoleum, curtains with industrial plastic blinds, and period fireplaces had been torn out and plastered over, leaving no sign that they had ever existed. All at once I understood why, for as we awoke each morning, we would see Freddie from our bedroom window walking to the bottom of his garden, where he would stop and look around, as far from the house as possible, shaking a large yellow duster above his head.

I tapped on Cecily's door and strained to hear her voice, but the only sound I heard was the voice of a T.V. gameshow host working himself up into a state of feigned excitement. I gently opened the door and looked into the room. I was never to forget the scene which etched itself on my mind on the afternoon of my first meeting with Cecily. She sat beside the far wall facing the window. In front of her a T.V. set stood on a small table. Against the near wall was a single bed. Freddie had made a simple device from lint and cotton wool which he would push under her chin to lift her head so that she could see the TV, but it had fallen into the tray which was part of her plastic bib so that her head had slumped forward, and her eyes were fixed on a small part of the yellow and brown pattern on the linoleum in front of her.

'Is someone there?' she asked in a nervous voice.

'It's me, your next-door neighbour,' I answered.

'What do you want?' she wanted to know.

'Just to introduce myself and ask how you are.' She uncurled a bony finger and pointed at the telly.

'Turn that thing off,' she said, 'and sit there on the bed.' As soon as the racket had faded, she asked, 'Did you say you'd come to see how I am? What do I look like to you? I've sat here in this chair for eleven years, staring all day long at that patch of lino with the stupid telly blaring all around the room. How do you think I am?'

I sat quietly for a moment, asking God for words to say, because I had none. Suddenly she spoke.

'Sorry,' she said. 'It's not your fault. It's good of you to come to see me. I don't get many visitors. Freddie's very kind but I do get so lonely. Now tell me, what made you come today?'

It was as if a door had opened, and I simply said, 'I think God sent me.' At that moment I had the strangest conviction that some sort of inexplicable spiritual connection had been made between Cecily and myself.

All at once Freddie knocked and called out, 'Hello, tea and biscuits!' He set Cecily's tea and biscuit down on her tray. 'She may need a little help,' said Freddie as he left the room. I watched as Cecily picked up her cup. Her fragile hands trembled hopelessly, and her tea spilled over into her bib. I reached out and steadied her hands, tilting her cup as carefully as I could.

'Would you like me to dunk your biscuit?' I asked, and there, in that sparse, lonely room something deeply mysterious was happening. Perhaps one of the oddest tea parties in all history was taking place. Here was I, once a pitiless parasite with concern for no-one but myself, guilty of sinking to abominable depths in pursuit of personal gain, and yet now delighting in the company of this woefully deformed elderly lady, so delicate, yet so physically diminished that her feet didn't even reach the floor but swung to and fro' like the feet of a child.

'Aren't you kind,' she said gratefully as I carefully placed the dry corner of the tea sodden biscuit between her fingers.

'Not me,' I told her, 'I'm not in the least bit kind. You wouldn't believe how unkind I've been, but there's someone else here with us. He is so very kind.'

She thought for a moment before asking, 'Who else is here? Who do you mean?" She strained to turn her head, trying to look around the room.

'It's Jesus,' I told her. 'He's the one who brought me here. Last year I gave my life to him. I said sorry for all the terrible things I've done, and he forgave me. He took the punishment for my sins and all the sins in the whole world when he gave his own innocent life on the cross. I thanked him from the bottom of my heart and asked him to live in me and control my life, and that's why I'm here. It's the honest truth. He wants you to know that he loves you and really cares about you. It was Jesus who helped you with your tea and dunked your biscuit, not me.'

Cecily sat quiet for a few moments and when she spoke, her voice was filled with wonder.

'I think that's just marvellous,' she said, 'But would you do something for me? Would you sit on the floor in front of me if you don't mind, just for a minute. Only I'm stuck here like this, and I'd like to see your face.'

That was the first of many visits. I would read and pray with her and explain as best as I could the passages we shared together. Her favourite chapter was John 10. She wanted me to read it again and again. She loved the picture of Jesus as the Good Shepherd who cared so much for his sheep that he would never abandon them, even when wolves attacked them and, in fact, was even ready to give his life to save them.

I called on her late one morning to find her strangely excited.

'I've got something to tell you,' she said in a whisper. 'After the nurse had bathed me today, and settled me in my chair, I did what you did. I said sorry for my sins and asked Jesus to forgive me and come to live in my heart, and he did! And I'm so happy! But I'm not telling Freddie because he wouldn't understand.'

I could tell some wonderful stories of how God enriched my life through my acquaintance with Cecily, and in recording this account I am grateful for the flood of memories which I treasure of that tender little soul who gave me so much, and from whom I learned the secret of true beauty, which the Apostle Peter perfectly describes in the third chapter and fourth verse of his first letter as, 'the unfading beauty of a gentle and quiet spirit, which is of great worth in God's sight.' (NIV)

Chapter Three

It was around this time that I was preparing for baptism, and my dear parents who had shed many tears and suffered many sleepless nights in prayerful pursuit of my wandering, lost and unworthy soul, travelled the two hundred and fifty miles from their home in North Wales to witness this miraculous event. Our lovely daughter and her brand-new husband were to be baptised on the same day and we were looking forward to a great time of family fellowship. Very rarely did I see our mother weep, but on that day, as I testified to the miracle of God's redeeming grace, I saw her in the front row of the church pressing her handkerchief to her eyes.

Stella had cooked a fine extra-large turkey and we shared a joyful meal together, the whole family gathered round an ancient farmhouse table. And after lunch, mother asked if she might visit Cecily, who had greatly enjoyed reading her autobiography, so we went next door and were very graciously welcomed by Freddie, who accompanied us to Cecily's room where we sat down together in a row on the bed.

After introductions and the mandatory pleasantries, mother, for some unknown reason, took it into her head to challenge me on the touchy subject of my addiction to tobacco.

'How are you managing, now that you've given up smoking?'

Her question came like an unseemly dark blot on a pristine sheet of pure white paper! The implication, of course, was that baptism must surely have extinguished those raging fires of hell which burn unceasingly in the tormented soul of a cigarette smoker. But I wasn't having any of it! Those choking rules and regulations which had defined my childhood notion of the Christian faith: 'Thou shalt not smoke; thou shalt not enter the doors of a dance hall; thou shalt not be found in a cinema,' along with many other laws and precepts, had aroused the rebel in me and driven me to search for a freedom elsewhere, a freedom which I had discovered was illusory, but which I had now tasted at last in the grace and power of the Holy Spirit.

'Who said I'd stopped smoking?' I asked defiantly. I haven't stopped! In fact, I'm smoking even more than before because I'm so excited all the time and cigarettes calm me down!'

When mother was on a mission her face assumed an expression of such dogged determination that strong men had been put to flight simply by the set of her jaw and the force of her character, which had, after all, taken her to the very heart of Africa in spite of her chosen mission's selection panel turning her down three times due to a heart defect! She was staggered by the body blow which I had so defiantly delivered, but she rallied after just a moment, gathered her commanding authority about her like a sergeant major who is accustomed to unquestioning obedience.

'But you'll just have to stop, lad!' she ordered in a voice which brooked no dissent. I saw that Cecily's hands were clasped tightly as though to stop them trembling, but I wasn't going to concede.

'Who says so?' I demanded.

'I do, I say so!' she answered.

'On what authority?' I wanted to know.

'The authority of the Bible,' she said. I had, of course, been expecting this and was quite prepared to fight my corner.

'Where in the Bible are we forbidden to smoke cigarettes?

Mother was ready with the verse, which I had heard used many a time in this context. She spoke in a voice charged with reverence, using her beloved King James translation presumably to add dignity and weight to the text,

'What? Know ye not that your body is the temple of the Holy Ghost?' She quoted the verse with solemn authority, adding the reference for good measure, '1 Corinthians 6 verse 19.'

'Ah, yes, we all know that verse and indeed the context, mother, which is specifically fornication. Sexual immorality. You'd be hard pressed to use it in connection with tobacco smoking without doing violence to the text. I want you to know, mother, that with the best will in the world, you are not my conscience. I have a new conscience. His name is the Holy Spirit. If you truly believe I should give up cigarettes, you'll need to pray that the Spirit of God will convict me. If and when he does, I give you my word that I'll stop.'

To my surprise I heard my father's voice. 'Amen,' he said quietly. But mother wasn't convinced.

'I still think...,' she began. I interrupted her.

'Tell me,' I said, 'What is the greatest of the commandments?'

She answered confidently, 'You shall love the Lord your God with all your heart and with all your soul and with all your mind and with all your strength.'

'Go on,' I prompted, 'and what comes next?'

'Oh, and your neighbour as yourself.'

'Now, mother, do you truly love your neighbour as yourself? Haven't you erected a six-foot high concrete fence between your front garden and his? Isn't that because you can't stand the sight of the man?'

It was true that the neighbour was rather trying and that any efforts to win him over had been disappointing, but patience had long been exhausted and the result was that harsh, dividing barrier.

'We need to address our minds and effort to the keeping of the greatest commandment,' I observed with the tone of a thorough going hypocrite, 'so that when the beam has been removed from our eye, we will see clearly to remove the speck from the eye of another.'

Later that day mother said to one of my sisters, 'My word, John gave me such a lecture today!'

My sister answered, 'It serves you right! He's getting his own back for all the earache you've caused him!'

She was right all along, of course! The truth was that I was gripped in the vice of nicotine addiction, and I simply didn't want to give the wretched drug up!

Chapter Four

We had sold our house and shop premises and moved across town. Because of the Bible knowledge which had been such an obligatory feature of my boyhood, and in spite of my innate unsuitability, I was called to be lay Pastor of a small village Baptist church just outside the city. It was there that God taught me the lesson of perseverance!

The baptistry had not been used for more than twenty-five years, and when a young university student asked to be baptised, I found that the baptistry was leaking and unusable. With the help of Gordon, our organist, a truly godly little man whose presence simply exuded the meekness and gentleness of Christ, we set about restoring the leaking ruins. We stood together in the old baptistry in our wellies staring at the stagnant water and the bulging tiles. We had discovered that the water wasn't leaking out, but rather leaking in! As the local water table rose with the rain, so did the water level in our baptistry! We had ordered a hefty fibre insert, but found it was too big.

'Do we know what we're doing?' I asked Gordon.

'Well no,' he told me.

'Well, that is, I don't either. But I shouldn't have spoken for you. That was quite wrong.' I said, 'So let's pray, otherwise we won't get anywhere. We've got less than a week to get this done!'

We stood close together with the water just below the top of our wellies and asked the Lord for his help. Despite what had appeared to me to be insurmountable setbacks, the work was finished late on Saturday afternoon. We cleared away our tools, rolled up the protective plastic sheeting, and filled the new baptistry with water.

As the light faded, we simply stared in total wonder at the work which God had achieved against all advice from the usual naysayers, with their warnings of floods and various other probable disasters. My dear brother Gordon had solved all the tricky technical problems which arose. In his usual self-effacing way, his brilliant solutions were always offered as modest suggestions which I seized upon with a gratitude which surprised him, since he truly believed that his contribution was of little value.

As darkness fell and we turned on the lights, I held my breath in awe as the crystal, clear water shimmered against the pale blue background of the new lining. We bowed our heads and gave grateful thanks to our creator God, the supreme builder and architect of his living church. The service which followed the next day encouraged and inspired the little congregation. We ended with that magnificent Wesleyan hymn:

> 'And can it that I should gain
> an interest in the Saviour's blood,
> Died he for me, who caused his pain,
> for me who him to death pursued!
> Amazing love, how can it be,
> that thou, my God shouldst die for me!'

Gordon crouched, trembling over our little organ and drew such passion and volume from that quivering old instrument that our small assembly of believers seemed to threaten the very fabric of the little building with the enthusiasm of their singing.

* * *

I had been pastoring the church for about two years. One Sunday morning I was out early with my dog, praying for the day's ministry. I was always very tense before a service, feeling hopelessly inadequate and utterly unworthy to be entrusted with the exposition of the word of God. I opened a brand-new pack of cigarettes and was just about to light up when the Holy Spirit spoke to me.

'Do you truly love me more than these?' he asked.

'Lord,' I shouted like a petulant child, 'That's not fair! I'm gasping!'

Once again, the Spirit of God had answered my mother's prayers. I saw no way of wriggling out of the challenge of verse 15 from chapter 21 of John's gospel. I was caught out by what most Bible students might see as my misinterpretation of this question which Jesus asked Peter. Perhaps my lifelong passion for fishing has led me into error in my understanding of the question which Jesus asked.

Eddie was in the same year as me at school. He was unusually gifted, intellectually; one of those students who seem able to grasp any concept instantly and store masses of complicated information in some copious compartment in his mind, with the ability to call upon it effortlessly and with perfect accuracy. Although not a studious pupil, he performed in examinations to a standard which was far above average and was expected to enjoy distinguished university success with the option of any career he might choose. Eddie's family owned a fishing boat, back in those days when, though fishing was a challenging and dangerous occupation, the harbour of our town was full of boats, a fleet of nearly forty vessels, most of which were managing to make an unpredictable living.

From an early age, Eddie would spend the school holidays going out to sea fishing with his family. It was a life of physical hardship which demanded total commitment. The working-day would begin at about two o'clock in the morning when the boats would leave the harbour in all winds and weather, returning after twelve or fourteen hours, where the catch would be sold at the quayside.

On his sixteenth birthday, Eddie caused consternation among the teaching staff by announcing his intention to leave school and join the crew of the family fishing boat. No efforts to dissuade him from taking this ill-advised step could bring about a change of mind. It was put to him that no career was beyond his aspirations and that the life of a fisherman would in no way do justice to his glowing prospects were he to reconsider and continue his education. But Eddie remained adamant.

'The fishing life is in my blood,' he told us. 'I'm no' interested in anything else.'

I remember seeing Eddie years later, walking home with his father and brothers in the late afternoon after a day's fishing, each wearing his heavy waxed dark blue jumper with its distinctive mother of pearl buttons on the shoulder. Sometimes they'd be whistling jauntily in tune together, a family joined in the indestructible fellowship of their love of fishing, out on the wild North Sea.

It would be difficult, if not impossible, for a theologian with no personal experience or love of the fishing life, to begin to understand the irresistible power of the call of Jesus when he challenged Peter to leave his cherished life, his boat, and that love of the open sea which is enshrined in the DNA of all true fishermen. Nor would it be possible to understand the cost which Peter, his brother and their companions paid as they pulled up their boats, left everything, and followed Jesus.

'We have left everything to follow you!' Peter was later to remind Jesus, perhaps a little ruefully, according to Mark 10 verse 28 (NIV).

John chapter 21 finds Peter, along with just six other disciples at what seems to have been a loose end. Judas, of course, was no more and four of the other disciples were occupied elsewhere. Peter's acknowledgement of 'Jesus as the Christ, Son of the living God' had been proclaimed by Jesus as the rock, or foundation upon which he would build his church, according to Matthew chapter 16 verses 17-18, but it would seem clear that Peter's denial of Jesus has left him out of his depth. The brash self-confidence he flaunted as he rebuked Jesus in Matthew 16 verse 22 is long gone. But at least he knows what he's doing in a fishing boat and it would be natural for him to return to the familiar reassurance of his first love.

I may, of course, be wrong, but I can virtually see him gazing longingly out across the sea of Tiberias, followed by a disorganised, aimless and depleted group of disciples who would doubtless be looking to him for leadership.

'I'm going out to fish,' he said, and the others readily went with him. The little group suffered the self-same frustrating disappointment as they had done on that day when Jesus first called them, according to Luke chapter 5 verses 1-11. On both occasions they toiled all night and caught nothing. It was only when Jesus intervened that they were rewarded with a truly miraculous catch.

On this occasion, when John saw the size and number of fish that they had caught he turned to look at the strange figure, obscure and mysterious in the early dawn light.

'It's the Lord!' he said to Peter.

Peter wrapped his cloak around him and leapt straight into the sea. He was no athlete, but he drove himself through the water, thrusting aside the clinging seaweed. When the others arrived, it was, of course Simon Peter who climbed aboard to claim the prize and drag the net ashore. The miraculous catch was laid out on the shore like great slabs of burnished silver glistening in the rising sun, and carefully counted.

'One hundred and fifty-one, one hundred and fifty-two, one hundred and fifty-three!' Fishermen's lifetime reputations are built on catches like this!

'Simon, son of John,' said Jesus.

Not Simon Peter! Not the one on whose divine revelation of the Christ the church would be built! No, no! the one Jesus addresses here is Simon, son of John, Simon the fisherman!

'Do you truly love me more than these?'

'Don't be afraid,' Jesus had told Peter those three years earlier as he had fallen on his knees, astonished by a net-breaking catch. 'From now on you will catch men.' So he had left everything and followed him. But now Peter had returned to his first love.

That was how I saw it on that Sunday morning, thirty years ago. My nicotine habit was an essential part of my old life, and I knew that the verse which the Holy Spirit used, and which came with such conviction and power out of nowhere, was urging me to surrender my habit to Christ. From that day on, I never smoked another cigarette.

I told the Lord, 'You have convicted me, and now you must give me strength to obey, because I've been such a passionate smoker for thirty-five years and I can't do this on my own.'

Epilogue

A footnote. 'Simon, son of John, do you truly love me *more than these*?' Would Jesus really have invited Peter to start bragging yet again about the superior quality of his commitment, compared with the other disciples? Was this not the very thing which Jesus deplored and for which he took his disciples to task?

A Day in Malawi
Introduction

When I visited Kambilonjo in the year 2002, first impressions were that it was a remote, chilly little village among the mountains, dominated by a massive mound of dark rock which towered above a cluster of houses, scattered haphazardly under its shadow. We had travelled 150 kilometres north from our base near Blantyre into the central district of Malawi. We had negotiated the tortuous dirt track which leads from the tarmac road to the village in response to an appeal from the local Pastor for help in caring for the many orphans and desperately needy children in the area.

Sometimes we had been forced to stop on the way and lend our weight to the task of heaving our truck out of yet another deep rut, filled with muddy water. You could take advantage of this break in your journey by posing for a mud-spattered photograph with your right foot planted in Mozambique, and your left foot in Malawi. The road marks the border between the two countries and has since undergone significant improvement. But in those days, especially during the rainy season, it was touch and go whether or not your four-wheel drive truck would actually make it to Kambilonjo at all. The muddy track was a treacherous network of ravines up to a metre deep and the 10 kilometres or so from the turn off at the tarmac road could take two hours of precarious, bone juddering negotiation.

Four years had passed since I had first set out for Africa on what has now proved to be a twenty-two year journey which has changed not only my life, but the lives of thousands of destitute children. Aquaid Lifeline is a charity which was founded under the direction of God and supported by the promises of his word. From the outset, funding came from a fledgling business, established and managed by my family, a family of erstwhile thorough-going sinners, redeemed, reborn and transformed by the grace and energy of the Holy Spirit. It reminds me of that wonderful story in 2 Kings chapter 7 where we're told that God chose to use four apparently deadbeat and worthless lepers to bring the wonderful news of a great deliverance to the starving city of Samaria!

Chapter One

Pastor Jingo was waiting to greet us, along with a group of women singing an enthusiastic welcome to the visitors. Jingo was a stocky little man who spoke in short, lively bursts. His wife was a gracious, hospitable lady who carried her son everywhere she went. Her technique was to take his weight on her hip while his arms were wrapped around her neck which meant that her steps were uneven, and her progress was awkward. The boy was about seven years old and was suffering, like so many, from cerebral palsy. Her devotion to her son moved me deeply, and when, three or four years later, he passed away, she was inconsolable.

We were surrounded by a large crowd of children who gazed up into my strange white face with an innocent fascination which made me feel like one of those rare captive animals, which we cage as exhibits in a zoo! 'Azungu!' they were muttering knowingly to one another which, I was told, literally means 'ghost'! I had seen many malnourished and ragged children during our travels in Malawi and I'm not sure if it was the bleak sense of hopelessness which I felt on my first acquaintance with Kambilonjo village that made this group of little children look so much more needy than the others I had already come across. There's something which stirs up a kind of indignation deep within when you're confronted by a three or four-year old with impossibly thin, ulcerated legs, a distended stomach and wispy orange hair, wearing nothing but a threadbare T-shirt with its faded, dusty image of a grinning Mickey Mouse. Old cast-off clothing, freely donated by people in the West, is big business in poverty-stricken Malawi. But how could I have dreamed that from this seemingly God-forsaken place would one day emerge so many living candles, burning like brave beacons of hope and grace in a dark place!

Pastor Jingo invited me to take a tour of the village. Followed by an entourage of more than fifty curious children, we were led through a cluster of tiny round windowless mud houses with grass roofs, some with an arrangement of old fertilizer bags hung across the doorway. There was a uniform sense of extreme poverty, because each house was totally devoid of the clutter of any personal possessions. A single blackened cooking pot, a small hand brush made from stiff grass and a battered water tin, its size determined by the age and strength of its owner. A few potatoes or three or four handfuls of maize and a small bunch of pumpkin leaves in a straw basket, and nothing else except for bedding, which was a grass mat, rolled up and leaning against a wall. No blanket, nor any comfort for the cold nights, no change of clothing, no footwear, except, perhaps, a tatty pair of flipflops for Sundays. Outside each hut was an arrangement of three blackened stones—this was the kitchen.

As we stopped to speak with the resident of one of these diminutive houses, three of the children pushed their way forward and went inside. The oldest was about seven, the youngest three. Father and mother had both passed away and the old lady, who was their last living relative, had been expected to take responsibility for them. Grandma didn't get up but sat leaning against the wall with her knees drawn up to her chin, her 'chitenje' carefully gathered round her ankles for the sake of modesty. I could see that dense cataracts had clouded her eyes, and when she tried to speak her voice seemed to be choked by a large goitre.

The Pastor spoke, 'She is greeting you,' he told me, 'She is apologising for failing to rise. She has great difficulty with standing due to a bad pain in her legs. These little ones are her orphans. She is the one who is looking after them and they are proud that you have visited their home. Malawians are honoured by a visitor.' Pastor Jingo held the fertilizer bags aside. The children were staring up at me. 'Muli bwanje?' (how are you?), I said.

They giggled with delight. 'Diri bwino,' (I am fine), they said in unison. There was an excited murmur from the rest of the crowd. 'The azungu is speaking Chichewa,' they were saying happily. I asked the Pastor how this family could possibly survive.

'We have an offering each week during our service,' he told me, 'and that's how we try our best to look after those who are poor and needy. Those who don't have money can give a little maize or a few potatoes, but there are so many, it's not enough.'

He wanted to show me the church which was built on a rock and painted white. There was a date etched into the wall behind the brick pulpit. '1919' the date claimed. I thought of the missionaries who had laboured, a century ago in this remote, inhospitable place. The corrugated iron roofing sheets had lifted at the edges as violent winds had torn them off and blown them away. The congregation had gathered them and done what they could to straighten them before somehow nailing them back until the next gale would come shrieking through the mountains and ravage again their precious church.

'When the rains come, water comes in,' the Pastor told me. He waved his hand towards the pews which were made of mud. 'We can't sit everywhere,' he explained, 'only in the dry places.' Outside was a cement lined pit, about 4 feet wide, 6 feet deep and 10 feet long with steps leading to the bottom.

'This is our baptistry,' the Pastor told me proudly. 'We are to have a service here this Sunday when I will baptise thirty-one new members. Yes, thirty-one,' Pastor Jingo repeated, 'And three months ago, I baptised twenty-seven. Yes, twenty-seven.'

I watched one of the three women walking across the rocky, uneven ground with that huge twenty-five litre tin of water on her head, balancing on a little wreath of dry grass. Her back was perfectly straight and her movements as she lowered her burden and emptied her water into that cavernous baptistry were a study of grace and elegance.

'Where does the water come from?' I asked the Pastor.

'Over there,' he answered, waving his hand vaguely. 'It's from the borehole, not very far.' But it was far! 'There will be others tomorrow, who will take their turn. In three days the water will be enough.'

No recompense or payment was offered to these women, who would toil from first light until evening to ensure that all was ready for the service on the following Sunday. I felt an uncomfortable flush of shame as I thought of my own eagerness to serve my Saviour in the early days of my Christian life, and of the comparative reluctance which had seeped into my daily life and sapped the energy of the Spirit in me. I have heard many western Christians deploring what they see as the shallowness of African believers. I would offer them a twenty-five litre container and ask them to toil from dawn until dusk for three days to fill a cavernous baptistry for no other reason than their love for Christ and their concern that he should be held in the highest honour.

Chapter Two

I was resolved to build a centre for those dear orphan children, a place of shelter, with food and clothing, a place where they could learn and run and play. The area chief, who was himself a believer, immediately offered a suitable tract of land with space for a large building to accommodate over 150 children, plus a large area for growing vegetables and maize, the Malawian staple diet.

So successful was the Kambilonjo maize harvest that the project was able to sell surplus food to our other centres. Some years later a Scottish family, the Dunphys, visited the centre with me. They brought along their two girls, one sixteen at the time, the other thirteen. They fell in love with Kambilonjo and its people, just as I had done. With the help of their home church and using donations from their family business, they finished the half-built orphan residence to a high standard and built a wonderful adventure playground and a fine health centre, which serves patients from a wide area, reaching out, even to Mozambique.

By the grace of God, and according to his unsearchable plans, Kambilonjo has been transformed from what appeared to me on first acquaintance to be a dead-end God-forsaken village, into a thriving community. Many of those skinny, ragged little orphans who followed me around on that day almost twenty years ago have graduated from various colleges, their fees graciously paid by the tireless Dunphy family and the loyal supporters of St Andrews Presbyterian Church, Arbroath. There have been accountants, teachers, and tradesmen.

I am, at this moment, looking at a photograph of one of the Kambilonjo orphans. His name is Chifundo Gwesere and he is standing in a white coat at the entrance of the University of Malawi College of Medicine. Chifundo is a brilliant student and has been appointed as President of the Medical Students' Association of Malawi. We built a large new church since the old building could no longer accommodate the growing congregation, but so many attended the official opening service we had to meet outside.

As we left Kambilonjo that day and went bumping and lurching towards our centre at Namisu, 150 km away, we made our plans for the new development. My strategy was never organised or carefully considered. I simply responded, not to logistical convenience, but to need, as God clearly revealed it. I had no restrictions nor concerns about planning consent. If a Pastor or a chief appealed for help, sometimes sending a list of two hundred or more orphans and needy children in his area, I would visit and we would hold a meeting when I would invariably be offered land for building and for growing food for the children and staff. Sometimes there could be a nominal cost for the land, but our promise to drill a precious borehole for clean, pure water for our children—which could be shared by the local community—would be taken into consideration.

In this way we have built twelve centres scattered around the southern and central regions of Malawi, caring for the physical needs, education and vocational training of more than 3,000 orphans and needy children in those exact places which were chosen, not according to any plans of mine, but according to need as God our Father made it known. Perhaps this lack of planning and consultation may seem irresponsible and cavalier to those who prefer to see all t's crossed and all i's dotted before setting out on such a vitally important enterprise. But I firmly believe that, unlike the disastrous wreckage of the schemes of Robert Burns' poor mouse, the 'wee sleekit, cowran, tim'rous beastie,' the plans of God never 'gang aft agley!'

Chapter Three

It was a relief finally to leave the dirt road and put on some speed! There were no 'safety' cameras in those days and the roads were almost deserted. The aim was to reach Namisu Village before dark because it wasn't all that unusual to meet vehicles with no lights! After a stimulating run, we arrived at the Balaka turn off where there is a police checkpoint. The policeman on duty had his back turned to us and appeared to be talking on the telephone, so we sneaked quietly by, feeling just a bit guilty. But as we turned onto the Zalewa road, two policemen stepped in front of our truck holding up their right hands. Held in the crook of their left arms, each of these officers of the law cradled an AK47 automatic rifle against his body. My heart sank as they approached. I began desperately preparing a speech in mitigation.

'We're coming from Kambilonjo, officer,' I would say. 'We're planning to build an orphan centre up there. We need to reach Namisu before dark, officer. Oh, by the way, next time you see my brother, police Sergeant Catchyole, give him my regards.' The sergeant was the son of Peter, a dear Pastor friend of mine, and he truly was a close Christian brother. But, mercifully, I had no need to trot out my pitiful appeal, endorsed by shameless name dropping because one of the officers addressed me with a polite salute.

'Good afternoon, sir,' he said, 'may we ask you to assist us?'

Although at that moment I was ready to do absolutely anything in my power to assist the police, I was quite unprepared for his astonishing request. He waved his hand and pointed out a group of a dozen men, huddled together at the roadside. 'These men are criminals,' he announced. 'As you see, they are safely chained together. They cannot harm you. They have appeared today at court in Balaka and have received prison sentences. Tomorrow they will begin to serve their time in various prisons depending on the severity of their crimes, but for tonight they will be kept at Senzani police unit which is thirty kilometres along the Zalewa road. Our problem is that we have no transport and would be most grateful if you could offer us a lift.' I turned to look at the sorry looking characters, sitting in the dust, each with his own little history, the hidden aspirations, the dark secrets and disappointments of his personal life, but now lumped inseparably together, wrist to wrist, ankle to ankle.

Fathers and mothers, brothers and sisters, even wives and children count for nothing here, nothing at all. Their police guards ordered them to climb into our truck. Like some ungainly creature with twenty-four uncoordinated legs the dusty mass tumbled and wriggled awkwardly until they were all sitting as comfortably as their manacles would allow. One officer sat on the tailgate, his weapon across his knee, while the other sat behind the cab, facing him. We had just set off, when all at once, my companion and right-hand man, John Kan'gombe, said quietly.

'Remember Moses Phiri!'

We had left the road on our way out and dropped Pastor Phiri off at his grandfather's house, promising to pick him up on the way home. If I left the road and set off into the bush, I thought, the guards may think I am planning some mischief, so I pulled up.

'I've arranged to pick up a Pastor on the way,' I explained, and they nodded their permission.

As Moses and his grandfather came out to meet us, one of the officers tapped at my window. I have often thought of the happenings of that day and realised why I fell so much in love with that country and its people.

'Pastor,' he said respectfully, 'Would you please pray for these men?' I got out of the cab and looked at my congregation. This kind of thing just doesn't happen where I come from, I thought!

'Good afternoon, gentlemen,' I began, nodding to John, a wonderful preacher and interpreter. 'I understand that you have stood before a judge today and been found guilty of breaking the country's laws. So now you are to be punished. That is what we call justice.'

I was aware of a mood of sullen resentment simmering in the hearts of my captive congregation. Some faces were downcast, while others deliberately looked away.

'You are thinking you are suffering enough,' I went on, 'without this religious azungu who has no understanding of what it's like to go to bed when your whole family is crying with hunger, telling us that we're getting what we deserve.' One or two looked at me and nodded imperceptibly.

'But don't think you are any worse than I am!' I went on. 'I too have stood in the dock, back in my own country, charged with a criminal offence. By the grace of God, I was spared from prison and made to pay a large fine.' They were listening now though their guards seemed less than comfortable.

'When we stand before a judge, here in this life, we have many secrets which he doesn't know about. If the court which tried my case had known all about every one of my misdeeds, I could certainly have gone to prison for a long time. You have been convicted of a crime and you have been found guilty but imagine if the judge who sentenced you today had known the details of all the offences you ever committed! Just think about that!' One or two sniggered uncomfortably, while others nodded.

'Well, gentlemen,' I said, 'today you got away with it, but a day is coming for every man when he will stand before God, the perfect judge, and nothing can be hidden from him. Have you all heard of Jesus Christ?' I asked. 'I know you have. He is God's one and only Son. His Spirit is speaking to you now, wanting you to know that he loves you. In fact God sent him to suffer the judgement and the sentence for all your offences. All of them! Although he was totally innocent, the sentence passed on Jesus, the Son of God, was not imprisonment, but death. So, like me, whatever evil you may have done, Jesus endured the death sentence in your place. When he spread his arms and his executioners nailed him to a cross and left him to die, he was saying, 'It's all my fault!'

'The Bible says, he carried our sins in his body on the cross. And he doesn't demand that you promise to try and behave yourself in future or follow some strict religious practice. He only asks you to repent, to admit honestly that you are a sinner, helpless to save yourself. He asks you to thank him for taking the punishment we all deserve, including these two police officers standing here, and he promises to give you a new life. He promises to give you power to follow him and obey his word. That's what he's done for me, and that's why he sent me here today with this good news.

'I want to thank these two officers for the opportunity to speak to you, and I want you to have the opportunity to surrender your lives to Jesus Christ.'

I asked Pastor Phiri to pray for that strange little congregation, and he poured out his heart in supplication for their souls. There was a rattling of chains as some clasped their hands and there were deep murmurings amongst them as the Holy Spirit touched their hearts. As Moses Phiri said his 'Amen' to the prayers, there was an earnest response from several of the prisoners and three or four raised their hands, shook their chains and called out 'Hallelujah!'

As we dropped the men and their guards at Senzani Police unit, some wanted to shake hands. 'Thank you, Pastor,' they were saying. 'And God bless you.' And so ended a day in Malawi, a land of deep spiritual awareness.

Where Are You Phil?

Introduction

On Saturdays the corners of Phil's mouth would be crusted with a dry yellow deposit and the whites of his eyes would be tinged with a kind of faded ochre. His face would be drawn and haggard, so that he seemed to be on the verge of collapse, yet his whole being quivered with an unnatural energy. His speech would be blurred and nonsensical, sometimes punctuated by raucous laughter, and at other times he would suddenly become threatening and aggressive. You wouldn't want to be a passenger in Phil's Ford Capri at the weekends. It wasn't just the smell of half-eaten takeaways decaying under the seats, or ground into the rear carpets by the feet of wildly carousing buddies. It was his breath-taking driving; he would weave through heavy traffic at death-defying speeds, in uproarious defiance of the flashing lights and an indignant cacophony of horns as he left a trail of angry motorists in his wake.

Chapter One

Phil was an addict. Each Friday he would visit a designated pharmacist to pick up his prescription, which was a plastic bottle containing fifty-six tablets to be taken, the label said, two at a time, four times a day. Phil would gulp down all fifty-six as fast as he could in about half an hour. I was introduced to him by a friend who thought Phil deserved a fair chance. I was told he was a willing worker who had a few problems, especially at weekends but that normally he was as good as gold and would happily do anything asked of him. Above all, I was assured, he had a rogue's sense of absolute loyalty.

'He may not be very bright,' said my friend, tapping his forehead, 'But he'd go through fire and water for you.'

I was a back-street motor trader at the time and with some misgivings I had employed him as a car cleaner and handyman. The truth is, he wasn't much good at either, so I found a way to occupy him as a driver. Phil seemed overwhelmed with gratitude for what was, to him, an unexpected promotion.

'I won't let you down,' he promised. 'I'll stand by you, through thick and thin!' A couple of weeks later my friend told me that Phil had been serving a year's ban from driving.

When I challenged him on the subject he feigned surprise and said, 'I thought you knew! Everyone else does! Besides, I get my licence back next month!'

I'm not clear how Phil seemed able to worm his way into my life, or how I became so aware of his background. I had met his father, a rather aloof and disappointed man who had passed away.

'My Dad had no time for me,' he said one day. 'I wish you'd been my father. Things would've been different.'

His mother was a tiny woman who doted on him. When I tried to ask for her help to wean him off his drugs problem she was fiercely indignant.

'Poor little beggar,' she said, 'Nobody understands him. What harm is he doing anyone? He ain't doin' needles. It's only a few pills. Lots o' folk take pills. I take pills myself!'

Phil told me his mother kept his stash of drugs in her handbag, and if the police called to search the house, she would simply pick up her bag and go shopping. Most of his friends were involved with drugs and when his mother died, he was left alone in the family council house. There was a constant stream of addicts coming and going and he willingly fell victim to the pernicious influence of a community which is hell-bent on self-destruction. Sometimes he'd come to my door, begging for help.

'I'm potless,' he'd say, 'Haven't eaten for a week! Ain't even got money for the electricity meter. The house is freezin' an' I'm starvin' to death. Lend us a tenner an' you'll have it back at the weekend.'

Stella would give him a plate of Newmarket sausages and beans on toast.

'You're a star, Stell', he'd say, giving her a smelly hug. 'I wish I 'ad a missus like you. Things'd be different then.' He'd wag a grubby finger at me and say, 'You just don't know 'ow lucky you are! Now, 'ow's about that tenner you promised?'

His behaviour became more and more trying. One morning he phoned me at about 2 a.m. 'Help me, help me,' he wailed, 'the rozzers are after me an' I've crashed my car. It's stuck in a ditch an' I'm hidin' from the Old Bill. Come an' get me out of this. I'm beggin' you. I'm in a phone box in Barton. Hurry up, they're on to me. The place is crawlin' with rozzers! I'll be hidin' in the bushes near the pub. Just drive slowly past an' I'll shoot out an' jump in your car!'

Stella turned over as I pulled on my trousers.

'Who was that on the phone, and whatever are you doing now?' she demanded

'It's Phil,' I told her. 'The police are after him. He's crashed his car and he's hiding in the bushes out in Barton. I'm going to pick him up and take him home.'

'You're as daft as he is!' she snorted, turned over and went straight back to sleep.

I drove out to Barton, a quiet village off the main road a few miles from Cambridge. Only God knew, of course, that within a few short years I would be called to serve for eleven years as lay Pastor in the little Baptist church on the High Street. It was during this time that the Lord taught me the much needed lesson of perseverance! I drove slowly into the heart of the village, nervously alert to the possibility of being stopped by the police and having to account for my kerb crawling around in the dead of night. I passed the pub at walking pace, straining my eyes for any sign of the desperate fugitive from justice who had told me he'd be hiding there.

I stopped at the duck pond and got out of the car. I stood there in the silence, breathing in the still night air as folk of good sense slept peacefully all around me in the gentle calm of that quiet little village. All at once an owl called from the dark trees in the vicarage garden across the road.

'Twit! Twit! Woooh!' said the wise old bird.

I began to laugh quietly to myself at the sheer absurdity of Phil's vivid description of his dilemma. Where was he, I wondered. What sort of mind-altering narcotic had induced such hallucinations? How would he cope with tomorrow, and did he really care?

'Where are you, Phil?' I said aloud as I drove home.

Chapter Two

Next time I saw him I told him not to contact me again. 'Leave me in peace, I can't help you. As long as you hang around with those wasters who are all killing themselves you've got no hope.' My wavering desire to try to help Phil evaporated. He was under the control of forces far too powerful to deal with. His addiction irritated me; he was a weak, ungrateful, self-indulgent junkie heading for oblivion.

I would sometimes drive past his house; grubby curtains, both up and downstairs were always drawn and the garden was a tangled mass of weeds littered with plastic bags, bottles and waste paper. His mother, despite what I had thought were her shortcomings, had been houseproud, and all had been kept clean and neat.

One day as I drove past his house, I saw Phil hurrying round to his back door. More than two years had passed since I had committed my life to Christ, and I felt that the Lord was pointing him out to me. A day or two later I called on him. He answered my knock after a third or fourth thunderous attempt to rouse him, and stared at me with bleary eyes.

'It's you, John! It's you! Thank God! I thought it was them rozzers again!'

He looked emaciated; his deeply lined face was framed by his long, straight greasy hair. He was wearing a grubby denim waistcoat which hung open, revealing his skinny torso and prominent ribs. His feet were bare and bony. I felt a great wave of regret and compassion sweeping over me. How could I ever have abandoned him? That's the sort of person he was. He just seemed to be so utterly vulnerable.

'The place is in a bit of a mess,' he said, 'But you can come in if you want.'

The stench in the living room made my eyes water; there were a number of thick patches of cat faeces which had been trampled into the carpet. He saw me staring at a pattern of blood spots on the wallpaper.

'That's Jenny,' he said. "She annoys me, shooting up all over the place!' I saw a shadow, flitting past the curtained window, followed by a furtive tap at the door.

'Scuse me,' he said. He picked his way between the deposits on the carpet, like a bomb disposal expert negotiating a minefield. He opened the door and whispered urgently under his breath, and the visitor drifted away past the window.

'Can't get a minute's peace here. They won't leave me alone!' he whined.

'Phil,' I told him, 'this place needs cleaning up. I can hardly breathe.'

'I know, I know, but what can I do? I try to tidy up and the next thing you know you get cats coming in from all over the place. You scrape up the mess and the very next day they've been in half the night muckin' the place up. Then there's Jen and Carl an' all that mob. Weekends they're in an' out like they own the place. I can't get rid of 'em, shootin' up an' crashin' out on the floor an' the settee, an' even upstairs in my mum's old room, bless 'er. You should see the state of the bathroom! It's the drugs, John, it's all got out of control. I was alright workin' for you. I loved it, an' I don't blame you for sackin' me 'cause I conned you about my drivin' licence an', like you said, I could've got you in trouble, but I loved workin' for you, honest, I loved it!'

He looked at me beseechingly, desperate for the sympathy he would have expected from his poor mother. I thought of those thrilling stories one hears about addicts being wonderfully delivered from the chains of their habit in a single moment. There, in that choking little room, darkened by the rancid evidence of the power of the one who comes only to steal, kill and destroy, I prayed silently for Phil's deliverance.

'Is there a Bible in the house?' I asked him.

'Bible? Yes, I've seen one somewhere. Do you want to see it?' he answered.

I nodded. He left the room and after some time he came back with a King James Bible.

'This was my granny's on my dad's side,' he informed me. 'Mum said we should keep it. He didn't leave us nothin' else!'

I found the book of Isaiah and turned to chapter 53.

'I'm going to read this and mark the page. I'm going to ask you to read it and ask God to tell you what it means and who it's about. I'm coming back tomorrow with Stella to clean this place up, and I'll be asking you what God has said to you about this chapter.'

As I read the passage, I could sense that eternal power breathing through the words of that great prophecy which has pointed so many to Christ our Redeemer. I handed the Bible to Phil and he took it carefully as though recognising that he'd heard something sacred.

'Don't forget,' I said gently. 'Read it for yourself and ask God to show you who these verses are about, and what it means for you. It's changed my life, Phil, and made me a new person.'

He looked into my face as though something had begun to dawn on him.

'You are different, I was wondering what it was,' he said. 'I promise you, I'll definitely read it.'

The next day, equipped with a bucketful of cleaning materials and deodorants, my long-suffering wife Stella and I set off on our mission of restoration. Phil greeted us with unabashed delight.

'I did what you said. I read the bit in the Bible you showed me. It's about Jesus, isn't it? Am I right, John? Shall I put the kettle on?'

I could see that Stella was aggrieved by the shocking state of the place.

'Phil, Oh, Phil,' she said sorrowfully, 'whatever would your poor mum say if she could see what you've done to her bonny house!'

She followed him into the kitchen, and I heard her voice calling out like a woman in anguish.

'Oh, no! No! No!'

I went to investigate the cause of her despair and saw that the worktops were covered with filthy paw prints, discarded takeaway containers and unwashed dishes, crusted with sour, mouldy leftovers. Two of the cupboard doors had been torn off and thrown on the floor. The remainder hung open, all empty, with not a single sign of any foodstuffs. An open tea caddy, smeared with fingerprints, revealed a few teabags, and as Phil picked up a grubby kettle, Stella snatched it away and spoke through gritted teeth.

'I wouldn't drink a cup of tea in this house for all the tea in China! I'm sick, just thinking about it!'

Phil at once assumed his wounded soldier act.

'I've done my best, Stell! On my life, I've done my best, but since I lost my mum, I don't have nothin'. Truth is, I've 'ad enough, Stell. I used to take my mum shoppin' every day. I know I used to moan about her, but she was all I 'ad. All my friends are junkies an' crack 'eads 'cept for you an' John. It's them what's messed the place up! What am I supposed to do? I feel like killin' myself! It's only the drugs that help me to forget everything!'

I saw a great mountain confronting Phil and doubted that he would ever manage to climb it. In spite of myself, I was overwhelmed with pity. Stella reached out and wrapped her arms around him and he buried his face in her shoulder and sobbed, just like a helpless child.

Chapter Three

We spent two days cleaning up Phil's house. He was so happy, so eager to help. We cleared the rubbish, scrubbed the carpet, washed the blood stains off the wall, and Stella bagged up the curtains, the sofa and chair covers, took them home and washed them. We re-fitted the cupboard doors and bought a box of groceries. Stella cleaned the fridge and filled it with soft drinks, cheese, milk, sausages and bacon. Each time a visitor called, 'on business' Phil sent them packing.

'Ain't 'avin no more to do with them wasters,' he would say proudly.

We both shared in his excitement and it was such a thrill for us to share the gospel with him and to demonstrate the love of Christ in a practical way. We prayed that he would truly commit his life to Jesus and find strength to resist the temptations which he had found irresistible.

I had been invited to speak at a service in a town about thirty miles away. It was to be a meeting focused on folk who had attended the church Sunday school or youth group, but who had drifted away. There was to be a week of outreach, culminating in a Sunday service. I invited Phil to come along, and he agreed. I had presented the gospel of grace to him as simply as I knew how, and he had listened respectfully. He had been fascinated by the prophetic wonder of Isaiah 53, and had understood the meaning of Christ's conversation with Nicodemus in the third chapter of John's gospel. I was careful not to try to force him into a commitment to Christ, but was a bit frustrated as I prayed and waited for the penny to drop!

It had been made clear to me that the focus of the service was evangelistic, and I spoke from 2 Kings chapter 5 which points to the humanly untreatable affliction of sin, the necessity of repentance, the promise of forgiveness and a new creation through faith in Jesus Christ. The service ended as I invited the congregation to pray a heartfelt prayer of response to the voice of the Holy Spirit.

As soon as we were alone, even before we set off for home, Phil said excitedly, 'I prayed that prayer, John! I prayed that prayer! I feel just wonderful!' He rubbed his open hands up and down his body, saying, 'I'm clean! I feel clean inside!'

We went home together and dear Stella was so thrilled. We all held hands and prayed for one another and for the future new life we would all share and our hearts were full, and God was there with us, Father, Son and Holy Spirit, and nothing would ever take away our joy.

Phil wanted to come with me to church on the following Sunday. I was a member of a large city centre church and arranged to meet him at the door. As he hurried along the pavement, I saw that he'd made a valiant effort to look his very best and he skipped up the steps of the church, reminding me of

Habakkuk chapter 3 verse 19, 'The Sovereign LORD is my strength, he makes my feet like the feet of a deer, he enables me to go on the heights.' (NIV)

As he shook hands with our minister at the end of the service, he said 'Thank you sir. You'll be seein' a lot of me now. I'm a new member of your flock!'

   'Delighted to see you,' said the minister. Outside the church Phil turned to me and said, 'Can't believe how good this feels! I wish I'd done this long ago. I'm a proper Christian! All them wasted years!'

The following Sunday I was to meet him again at the church doors. I was so looking forward to seeing him again and hearing news of his week. But he was cutting it fine. The clock was ticking. 10.30 a.m. came and went, the church was full, the service had begun. I could hear the sound of the first hymn, but I couldn't seem to move. Perhaps he'd overslept or been held up somehow. Surely, he'd come! I'd see him, any minute now hurrying along the pavement, just as he'd done the week before. I stood waiting until 11 o'clock, as forlorn as a love-sick teenager who's been stood up!

   'I'm so sorry, Lord!' I said and went home.

After lunch I went round to his home. The curtains, which Stella had washed and ironed, were drawn again. I thought of that day 2,000 years ago, recorded in John chapter 6 (NIV), where the text of verse 66 says, 'From this time many of his disciples turned back and no longer followed him.' The chapter begins with a great crowd of five thousand followers, and ends with only twelve, one of whom, Jesus says, is a devil.

Verse 67 has always touched my heart. '"You do not want to leave too, do you?" Jesus asked the twelve.' I knocked on Phil's door and called his name.

His neighbour, who was in his garden said, 'You're wasting your breath. He's out with his mates.'

Two or three days later, I called again. I told myself that this was to be the last time. I wanted to know if the new life which Phil seemed to have embraced so enthusiastically had been a sham. He answered the door and invited me in.

'Sorry about Sunday,' he said. 'I 'ad a bit of business in Bedford. I'll be with you next Sunday, one hundred percent, guaranteed!'

He had barely finished speaking when the first of several visitors tapped at the back door. I listened as he mumbled and whispered, no doubt arranging for his furtive visitor to call back later.

'What are you doing to yourself?' I asked.

'It's not me! They won't leave me alone! I'm stuck 'ere by myself all day with nothin' to do!' He was shouting with feigned indignation. 'Look at my life, just look! 'ow would you like to be me? Ain't 'ad a job since I worked for you. That's my trouble, nobody wants me since I lost my Mum. Who's goin' to give me a job? Who? Nobody. that's who! I've broke in next door an' done my neighbour's meter. I've just finished six months unpaid community work a' now I'm due in court for even doin' my own meter! I'm a sittin' duck 'ere. If I was out at work all day they couldn't get to me, but it's 'opeless. I've 'ad enough! I feel like toppin' myself!'

'I'll get you a job, Phil,' I said quietly. 'I know someone who'll take you on. I think you're right; if you had a good, steady job with a decent wage you'd be set up. You could make new friends and keep in touch with Stella and me.'

He was looking upwards with a faraway expression on his face as though he was imagining an impossible dream. Before he could speak there was a sharp tap at the window. He sat upright with a start and hurried to the door. I heard him speaking in an angry, decisive voice, before shutting the door with a bang.

'Could you really get me a job, John? Are you sure?'

'You'll need to pray for me,' I said. 'We'll see what God will do.'

* * *

One of the deacons at the church where I was a member was chairman of a large company which had two thriving branches in town. The business included a large depot which stocked builders' supplies, and a timber yard. I drove to the site where the head office was situated, went to reception and asked to see the chairman.

'Do you have an appointment?' the receptionist wanted to know. 'You won't be seen without an appointment.'

It was time for one of those 'arrow prayers'. Our Mother used them often. 'Now, Lord,' she'd say, when confronted with an awkward situation.

'Could you just give the chairman my name, please. I assure you, he'll want to see me,' She looked unconvinced. 'It's Searle,' I said confidently. 'John Searle.' She buzzed through to the chairman's secretary.

'There's a Mr John Searle asking to see Mr Ridgeon. No, I'm afraid not. He doesn't have an appointment.' She put the phone down and looked at me doubtfully. A moment later the chairman's secretary came through into the reception.

'Would you come this way, please.' she said politely.

'Thank you, Lord,' I said under my breath as she led the way into David Ridgeon's office. He looked rather different, somehow, from our charming and modest church deacon. With branches all over East Anglia, David was responsible for a large workforce and as he invited me to take a seat opposite him, I was aware that his gleaming mahogany desk separated us.

'John,' he said, 'What a lovely surprise!' He stood up, leaned over his desk, and held out his hand.

'He's got such a kind face!' I said to myself as he asked, 'Now to what do I owe this considerable pleasure?'

'I'm here on an errand of mercy,' I began. 'I have a very needy friend who's desperate for a job.'

His face seemed to cloud over, just a little. He was an employer who valued harmony in his workforce and many of his staff had happily settled in a job for life with his company.

'Tell me about your friend. Is he a tradesman?' David wanted to know.

'Not exactly, but he did once work for me, and he's very willing. I found him very eager to please. He'd do anything asked of him. Some sort of unskilled labouring job would suit him.'

David was nobody's fool. His hands were locked together on his desk and he leaned forward ever so slightly.

'I presume he has issues, John,' he said, raising his eyebrows a little.

'Ah, yes, I'm afraid the poor chap has had a drugs problem, but he's made a profession of faith and we're trying our best to deal with his problems. He needs some order in his life and he's just desperate for a regular job.'

David looked dubious, giving the impression that this interview wasn't going very well.

'We're all one big family here, and I'm concerned that a drug addict wouldn't fit in. Tell me, John, does this friend of yours have a criminal record? As you know, we carry a great deal of valuable merchandise here. I'm no expert in these matters, but I understand that drug addicts may sometimes do absolutely anything to feed their habit. Does he. by any chance, have a criminal record?'

My heart sank. I had rashly promised Phil that I'd find him a job and here I was, on the verge of not only failing him, but compromising my relationship with a Christian brother. If I were to walk out of there carrying the burden of David's perfectly reasonable refusal the inevitable embarrassment for both of us would cause unspoken resentment. It is in such insidious ways that the enemy of the human soul works.

'The honest answer, David, is 'yes'. He broke into his neighbour's house and robbed the electricity meter. His sentence was six months unpaid community work.'

My dear Christian brother nodded.

'And is there anything else I should know?' he asked. 'I'm afraid so,' I said sadly. 'The last time his own meter was checked it was found damaged and empty. He's awaiting a court hearing for that offence.'

David sighed and said, 'Sounds like a hopeless case, John.' His voice carried a tone of finality, and who could blame him! But I couldn't give up on Phil.

'Yes,' I agreed. 'He does sound hopeless, but the truth is, he's helpless. He needs help.'

'Oh dear, Oh dear! You're putting me on the spot John. I don't quite know what to do. How does one deal with a situation like this?'

I could see that he was in a dilemma.

'You choose to deal with it as a business man, or as a follower of Jesus,' I said. 'My needy friend may well turn out to be an asset or a disaster as an employee, but your conscience will be clear.'

David picked up a 'phone and said to his secretary, 'Send up the wood yard foreman, please.'

Chapter Four

I called around to give Phil the news. 'You've got a job at Ridgeon's. Report to the wood yard foreman at eight in the morning. Don't be late, and don't let me down. Let them know when your court case is due, and they'll give you time off.'

His eyes welled up and spilled over. Tears streamed down his face. He spread his arms and said, 'Saved, I'm saved. I'll never let you down! On my life, John, I'll never let you down.'

A couple of weeks went by and Phil, in spite of earnest promises, didn't turn up at church.

'I'm readin' my Bible an' prayin' every day,' he told me, 'I couln't sleep at night without sayin' my prayers!'

I asked him how his job was going and he was less than enthusiastic.

'That foreman don't like me,' he said. 'I asked 'im if I could learn to drive the forklift an' 'e said, 'No chance.' Not only that, 'e moans if you're a few minutes late, but the worst thing is, by the time I've walked 'ome I don't 'ave no more'n fifteen minutes for my dinner before I'm walkin' back to work.'

Our neighbour Freddie, an elderly gentleman who was charmed by my wife Stella, had presented her with a beautiful old gent's Raleigh bicycle which he'd bought new many years before. It was impeccably maintained, and it was obviously something of a sacrifice, since Freddie was rather proud of its pristine green and gold paintwork and the satisfying tick, tick, tick of the running gear as its rider bowled along.

Stella, who loves all things vintage, had merely admired the bicycle one day, and the following day, dear Freddie had made a gift of it, happy in the understanding that it would be cherished. I explained Phil's transport dilemma, and Stella, somewhat reluctantly offered to loan the cycle to him until he could save enough to buy his own. She handed it over with strict instructions to keep it locked, making sure that it was clearly understood that she had been entrusted with the precious cycle and that she would expect it to be returned in as short a time as possible.

I called on Phil several times over the next three or four weeks but there was no answer either to my knocking or my shouting through the letter box. One Saturday I drove past his house and saw one of his friends disappearing round to his back door. I parked my car and ran round after his visitor whom I'd recognised as a paid-up member of the local drugs scene. As Phil answered my knock at the back door, I heard the front door shut as his old friend vanished.

'Hello, John!' he said with that exaggerated bonhomie which you often hear from people who've had too much to drink. 'Long time no see. I've been wonderin' where you were.'

He seemed to have lost any feeling or control of his tongue so that his diction was made sloppy with saliva which was coloured with that all too familiar yellow tinge.

'You're all doobed up, Phil. What are you doing?' I asked in despair.

He licked his lips. 'I've only 'ad a couple of pills, John. On my life, just one or two. They're legit. They're prescription drugs. I'm supposed to take them!'

'So how's the job going?' I asked.

'Don't talk to me about Rigeons,' he snarled. 'They gave me the sack. I couldn't manage heavy work like that! They 'ad me workin' like a slave, makin' me pick up that an' carry this. Then when I done my back in an' took a week or two off to recover, no sooner did I go back there than they asked for a doctor's line an' when I didn't 'ave one they fired me on the spot.'

'Where's the bicycle, Phil? What can I tell Freddie and Stella about the bicycle?' He laughed idiotically.

'Someone nicked it! What do you expect in this poxy town? It's crawlin' with bike thieves!'

I moved towards the door.

'No, no, John! Don't go! Don't leave me like this! I can't 'elp it! Sit down, sit down John an' I'll put the kettle on. I need you, John! You're my saviour!'

Little sprays of spittle scattered round the room as he spoke. I swear my heart was breaking as I turned my back on him and went out an shut the door behind me.

'Tell me, Lord, please, just tell me—what was I supposed to do!'

Chapter Five

I never saw Phil again, but about two years after I had been appointed as lay Pastor to Barton Baptist Church, he 'phoned me one Saturday afternoon.

'John, it's Phil. Can I ask you to do me a big favour?' His voice sounded urgent and sharp. I didn't answer, because I didn't know what to say. 'You there, John?' he snapped, sounding cross. 'It's important!' I'd never heard him sounding so focused, especially at the weekend.

'Are you alright, Phil? You sound like you're in trouble.'

He answered in an indignant falsetto. 'It's not me,' he squealed. 'It's a friend. She needs your 'elp. There's no-one else! I told 'er you're the one to save 'er like you done to me!'

My heart sank and I was sorely tempted to cut him off and hang up.

'Whatever are you screaming about, Phil?' I demanded. 'Just calm down and talk sense.'

He at once assumed the tone of a pleading supplicant.

'It's Cathy,' he said, his voice trembling with reverent emotion, 'You don't know 'er, but she's a lovely girl, an' she wants to get married!'

I confess that I burst out laughing. 'Congratulations, Phil.' I said sarcastically, 'When's the big day?'

He shouted angrily down the 'phone, 'Nah, nah! It's not me. I ain't marryin' nobody. She needs to marry 'er boyfriend an' there's no time to waste. You got to get it done quick! She's standin' right 'ere beside me. I'll put 'er on.'

Before I could protest I heard a girl's voice saying, in a strong Welsh accent, 'Hello, my name's Cathy, Cathy Williams.

Would you please perform a wedding ceremony for me and my boyfriend. We want to get married, see. Phil said you're a good man and a Baptist Pastor. Only I was baptised when I was sixteen, so I'm a proper Christian. My boyfriend isn't baptised, but he's a true believer.'

'Where were you baptised?' I asked.

'It was four years ago, in Wales. I've got a certificate to prove it, somewhere,' she said hopefully.

'So why,' I wanted to know, 'don't you get married in your own church in Wales, with all your friends and family around you?'

There was a short silence before she answered.

'They wouldn't come, see. Not now. They wouldn't want to know. They don't approve. They don't like Alex. Sorry we're in such a rush only we've just come back from Amsterdam and we've had no time to make arrangements, but I've got a ring. It's nothing fancy, not even gold, really. But what's important is that we get married in the sight of God. That's all that matters to us.'

I prayed a prayer. It came from deep in my heart; the truth is, I didn't know what to say. All at once the whole situation became clear.

'Is Alex dying in hospital?' I asked.

'Yes,' she answered, 'It's HIV. He's only got a few days at the most.'

Everything fell into place. This was another world. It was Phil's world, a world of infected needles, hepatitis and HIV, a world which no-one can really understand unless they live in it, and a world from which so many never escape.

'Listen, Cathy,' I said. 'Marriage isn't some slapdash on the spot arrangement when someone repeats a few magical sentences. There are arrangements to be made, witnesses must be present, and a registrar must be in attendance to ensure the ceremony is legal. These things apply even in a registry office. But I promise that I'll visit Alex in the morning, first thing, and we'll see what can be done.'

Cathy told me the ward number where I'd find Alex and we arranged to meet the next morning. I worried that I was out of my depth and spent some time in prayer that night asking for wisdom and guidance. As I approached the hospital the next morning just before eight o'clock, I saw a young woman walking alone in the opposite direction. She was leaning forward, carrying a heavy rucksack and she was wearing grubby trainers, jeans and a combat jacket at least two sizes too large. Could that be Cathy? Surely not! Cathy was waiting for me at the hospital. She wouldn't abandon Alex now, would she?

The ward was on the tenth floor. I pressed the bell, but nobody came. After the third long ring a nurse, who was obviously very busy, hurried down the corridor and opened the door.

'Yes, what is it?' She sounded rather impatient.

'Sorry to bother you, but I've called to see Cathy Williams and her fiancé, Alex. I'm a Pastor. They wanted to discuss their wedding ceremony.'

She looked at me as though she didn't believe a word I'd said.

'Well, whatever you want, you're too late. Miss Williams has gone. Her boyfriend died at two o'clock this morning.'

'Oh, what a world we live in Lord,' I said to myself as I dashed to my car. 'Who cares for these people? Where has that poor girl gone? What's to become of her?' I drove flat out along the deserted road away from the hospital, only slowing down when I passed the speed cameras. 'She must be at Phil's house, I thought. Sure to be.' I banged at the door and yelled through the letter box. No answer. Nothing!

'What are you doing?' I asked myself. 'Who do you think you are? Don't you realise that you can't save and deliver people?'

I'd prepared for the two services to be held that day.

'Just get home, calm down and trust the Lord to help you with your work,' I told myself. But I found it so difficult to entrust Cathy and Phil and their wretched world to Christ. I told the congregation Cathy's story and asked them to pray with me, but I couldn't speak. We all sat silent, and I wondered what we were all thinking. God gave me the grace to persevere in the ministry for another nine years and in spite of errors of judgement and a stubborn spirit, he blessed the work as he made preparation for the many challenges to be faced in Africa.

Epilogue

A year or so had passed since I had heard from Phil that one last time. I often thought of the day he committed his life to Christ and his joy and touching enthusiasm for Jesus which was so endearing. I wondered if the Lord had really let him go, or whether some day he might look me up, like the lost boy returning home. Then I came across an old acquaintance who wanted to talk about days gone by.

John at the time of Phil's story

We mentioned the names of one or two characters we'd known, when I said, 'Talking of characters, what about Phil? I wonder what he's up to!'

'Haven't you heard?' my old friend said. 'He's dead. Died in his bath, all on his own. According to the pathologist, he lay there for three days before he was found.'

I turned away and groaned inwardly. As I drove home, I kept asking, 'Where are you, Phil, and Cathy, where are you?' There is only One who knows the answer, no-one else.

Part Two
Reconstructed Stories
from Fact

The Renewal

Introduction

Aaron Fleming, local pest controller to Braxham Parish and estate gamekeeper to Squire Cawdrey of Grandsby Manor, stood at the gate of the rectory garden. He turned and looked at the clock, set in the church tower. 'Two o'clock, then, all but five minutes,' he muttered and took a deep breath. Why had he let himself in for this assignment he wondered? And should he really be wearing this uniform? After all, the war had been over for ten weeks or more and he was trying to pick up the threads of his life and find some relief from the haunting dreams which seemed to invade his consciousness without warning. It was just that the vicar would be expecting to see a soldier. His son, Second Lieutenant Craig Muir, had been a junior officer in the Suffolk regiment, although not in the same battalion as the Lance Corporal. He looked around the deserted village, feeling awkward and uncomfortable in his infantryman's tunic with the marksman's insignia sewn onto his left cuff and the single stripe of a Lance Corporal high on each arm.

Chapter One

As Aaron set out along the cinder drive which led through the garden to the rectory, a flurry of rooks rose from the trees behind the gloomy stone house, cawing loudly and scolding one another. He watched them as they wheeled and circled, landing again in the bare trees where they squabbled loudly over the best roosting perches. He blinked and shook his head. In spite of himself, his body tensed: he stood quite still and with narrowed eyes peered intently around the perimeter of the garden. As if in a dream, he saw clearly a cratered battlefield with scattered stumps of blasted trees which stood like forlorn monuments. He remembered vividly his first sniping duty, entrusted to him because of his legendary marksmanship. Sent to an outpost beyond the lines, his mission had been to disable an enemy machine gun post. He'd crawled along the shallow trench for 100 yards using elbows and knees to his sniper's hole, rifle held out before him, and settled down to wait. His breathing was calm and controlled as he lay calm and still, lost in single-minded concentration as though waiting for a marauding fox which had been causing havoc among the squire's pheasant chicks.

At regular intervals the air would erupt with the sound of machine-gun fire as an arc of shells spat fear at the allied lines. He saw that a helmeted head would appear for a brief moment as the gunner reloaded, then disappear as he sank out of sight like an animal going to ground. Aaron fixed his sights upon nothing but the space where the helmet had appeared and waited. He would have only a fraction of a second to find his target, but it was to be enough. A dark flicker of movement and he squeezed the trigger of his rifle. The helmet with its distinctive spike flew spinning upwards, one hand reached out as though waving farewell and fell out of sight, followed by silence.

* * *

Reverend Ambrose Muir stood at a window overlooking the rectory garden. A grey woollen cardigan hung loosely on his rounded shoulders. His watery blue eyes peered out from beneath bushy brows and a small bunch of wispy curls sprouted from each ear. His back was slightly bent, giving an impression of resigned weariness as he took a watch from his trouser pocket and peered at the time. He was waiting for the visitor he had invited for afternoon tea, Lance Corporal Fleming, in the hope of hearing, news, any news, of the last days of his son.

He withdrew a folded paper from his cardigan pocket. His hands shook as he opened the telegram and once again read the impersonal script, 'SECOND LIEUTENANT CRAIG MUIR : MISSING IN ACTION.' He had read the words countless times over the past months ever since the regiment's engagement at the battle of Arras with its tragic mass of losses. He folded the telegram away and turned to look at one of the photographs on the mantelpiece. An athletic youth wearing running spikes, shorts and a vest looked back at him, holding a silver cup above his head with both hands. A shock of unruly fair hair and an eager smile added a sense of energy and optimism to the image. A simple inscription read,

WINNER : 100 YARDS: OXFORD v CAMBRIDGE : 1912

'How could he be so utterly lost?' the vicar asked himself. 'What and where is my son's place in that faceless multitude of casualties?' Despite repeated enquiries, the war office had seemed unable to give any definite details of the missing Lieutenant's final action at the battle of Arras.

He turned to look again across the garden and, as the mantel clock struck two, he saw Lance Corporal Fleming, his visitor, standing stock still like a man in a trance. A gust of winter wind chased a light dusting of powdery snow briefly across the lawn and the Lance Corporal shook himself and blew into his hands as he walked briskly towards the rectory door.

The vicar's housekeeper was a gaunt, upright woman with a powerful jaw line, deep set eyes and iron-grey hair swept severely back into a tight bun. Before Aaron could offer any reason for his visit she spoke in an abrupt voice.

'This way!' Then she turned on her heel and walked briskly across the entrance hall, stopping at a door and knocking sharply. Aaron heard the vicar's voice which echoed as though coming from far away.

'Enter!' and as the housekeeper showed the Lance Corporal into the room he said, 'And bring tea and biscuits, please Agnes.'

It was an unhappy room: Aaron felt hemmed in by the dark furnishings. A towering bookcase filled with leather bound volumes covered one wall and a heavy mirrored sideboard occupied another. There were some framed sepia photographs set out on the sideboard.

'Good afternoon, kind of you to come.'

The vicar crossed the room, held out his hand and glanced briefly at the Lance Corporal. He seemed at a loss as to what to do next and distracted himself by picking up one of the photographs and offering it to his visitor for inspection as though it held some historical clue or explanation for the visit. Aaron, aware that the photograph must have some significant meaning, peered closely, despite some embarrassment at the image of a small wedding group, standing at the doors of a church. The groom, elegant in a morning suit, was half-turned towards his bride, looking into her face, totally ignoring the entire world, including, of course, the photographer who had doubtless been fussily issuing instructions to, 'Look this way, please, look this way!' This was the image of unabashed adoration the vicar had insisted on keeping as a memento of his wedding day in spite of his bride's embarrassment. Lance Corporal Fleming looked at the photograph. For some reason he felt a strange urge to salute!

'My late wife.' The Reverend Muir's voice choked with suppressed emotion. 'Our wedding day. Such an enchantingly gentle and beautiful woman. All who met and knew her loved her.' He drew Aaron by the sleeve to the window to give him a clearer view of the picture.

'She couldn't cope with life any longer when the telegram came,' he went on. 'She was quite lost, wondering where he might be. She seemed to be wandering in another world. This life became a burden to her. Her only purpose seemed to be to search him out, somehow. She would simply insist that he must be somewhere. She would disappear without anyone knowing where she'd gone to and the worrying thing was that several times she'd been seen down by the river and I would hurry down there to find her and bring her home. We used to enjoy a reading and daily prayers together, but she'd lost her reason and with it, her faith, I fear. We had hoped the tablets would be a help, but alas...'

The vicar drew a deep breath, like a child that has cried itself to sleep. Aaron, who had seen multitudes of dead and dying soldiers, laid out rank on rank after yet another futile assault on the enemy lines, had long ago learned to close his mind to pity, a common state amongst so many in the trenches. For the first time he began to understand something of what these lives, so carelessly lost, had meant to bereaved families. He felt agonising pity for the Reverend Muir as a tear welled up in his eye until it overflowed and rolled down his cheek, making its way through a small patch of bristles which his razor had missed that morning.

* * *

To Aaron's great relief the door opened and Agnes the housekeeper came in with a tray. The Reverend Muir and Aaron sat facing each other across a low table.

'So very good of you to come,' said the vicar. 'I do so much appreciate a visit from a soldier of the Suffolks, especially one who experienced that dreadful battle of Arras. That's where our boy was lost apparently.'

He poured the tea and offered the sugar bowl and the little milk jug. Aaron was about to take a first sip when the Reverend Muir said quietly, 'Shall we give thanks?' Aaron nodded.

'Gracious God,' said the vicar in a voice which he saved especially for such occasions, 'We thank Thee for these Thy mercies and ask Thy blessing upon them, even as we share Thy bounty, Amen.'

Aaron mumbled an indistinct 'Amen.'

The clergyman said quietly under his breath, 'Excuse me a moment.' He pushed himself out of his chair, took the victorious photograph of his lost son from the mantelpiece and placed it on the tea table, facing the window as though wishing to share the companionship of the afternoon with him. The vicar watched the face of his guest closely as though hoping to see a flicker of recognition on the Lance Corporal's face, but the visitor only looked briefly at the picture, turning it a little towards him in order to read the caption.

'Do you have a faith?' asked the vicar. 'I don't recall seeing you in church.'

'Sundays are busy days for me, Reverend, just like they are for you. It's when the squire holds his shootin' parties.' And as if to assure his host that they were on the same side he said, 'But I am a believer, Reverend. Truly, I do believe!'

He patted his breast pocket, where he kept a small New Testament. 'Wouldn't 've been without this out there at the front,' he said confidently. Men's lives 've been saved carryin' this.' He took the little book from his pocket and laid it on the table.

'Could I share a story, with you Reverend, concernin' a book just like this. Reckon Lieutenant Muir'd like to hear this account.'

The vicar hesitated a moment, then nodded. 'Do go ahead, please.' He reached out and pressed the switch of a standard lamp so that the strange scene was bathed in a circle of light; the ageing clergyman who looked so diminished that his clerical collar hung loosely around his neck sitting at the tea table waiting for the Lance Corporal, so recently returned from the killing fields of France, to tell his story. The vicar thought of the destruction and pain which had brought them together.

Chapter Two

'It was like this, Reverend,' Aaron said. 'We'd been shelling the enemy lines with our big guns for more'n twelve hours. That's how we knew we was goin' to make an assault. We was all tense an' nervous an' ten of our platoon was huddled in a foxhole waitin' for the bombardment to stop, an' then it'd be over the top for us.

'There was a Private in our platoon, Reverend, called Eddie Watts, a quiet sort o' lad but some of us used to rag 'im somethin' awful. It was 'cause 'e weren't like us, vicar. Every day 'e'd find somewhere to say 'is prayers; 'e'd kneel down, out of the way, close 'is eyes, put 'is 'ands together an' talk away as if there was someone there. Then 'e'd take 'is book from 'is tunic breast pocket an' read it. Some of us would torment 'im.

'But on this particular day we weren't in no frame o' mind to sneer an' scoff about the subject o' Private Watts religious 'abits. We knew that in less'n twenty-four hours we could all be dead. Some of us'd written letters home, just in case. One of Eddie's worst tormentors was Private Jack Pidley. 'E 'ad a vicious blasphemin' tongue in 'is 'ead, Reverend, but e'd gone real quiet. 'E just sat with 'is 'ead in 'is 'ands, an' now an' then e'd sniff a loud sniff an' blow air out of 'is mouth.

'Eddie went an' sat beside 'im, gave 'im a nudge an' asked 'im didn't 'e want to write to anyone. Jack said 'e'd never learned to write 'n' read. Couldn't see the point 'cause no-one gave a toss what 'appened to 'im. Eddie said 'e'd a spare piece 'o paper an' if Jack told 'im who to write to, 'e'd put down what 'e wanted, but Pidley said there was no-one, not no-one in the world what 'e cared about or what cared about 'im. Then Eddie came out wi' it!

'"God cares about you," e' said, "It's all 'ere in this book. It says God loves us."

'We was all listenin', Reverend, things weren't normal, you understand 'cause it's different when you know you'll soon be out there wi' them shells an' bullets whistlin' all round you. Private Billy Macready who'd always a lot to say for himself, spoke up.

"'Was I hearin' things?" he demanded. "Did you say what I thought you said? God loves us, was that it? Well, all I can say is 'e's got a funny way o' showin' it! Besides, if I was God, I wouldn't even like me, never mind love me, an' I definitely wouldn't love Jack Pidley, nor any one of us, includin' you! Ain't none of us worth nothin' an' that's why we're all in for the chop!"

"'You're quite right," Eddie answered, "an that's the very reason this little book's tellin' us that he loves us." Aaron opened the New Testament, found John's Gospel, turned to chapter three and read verse sixteen in a confident voice:

"'For God so loved the world that He gave His only begotten Son, that whosoever believeth in Him shall not perish, but have everlasting life." (AV)

"'If you want to know if God loves you or not, just look at the cross," Eddie went on. "That's where Jesus, his Son, gave his life in place of our lives, nailed there like a criminal while the whole world laughed and scoffed at him. He was innocent but he suffered the punishment for all those things we've done wrong. That's how much God loves us; that's how much he wants to forgive us. All we need to do is admit we've done wrong things, say sorry and ask him to give us a new heart an' a new way o' thinkin' an' behavin'. It's called bein' born again. I know we're all goin' to die, whether today or tomorrow or maybe in fifty or sixty years, but the new life God gives to anyone who believes in his Son 'll last for ever an' ever."

"'Are you tryin' to tell us," demanded Private Macready, "that even though we're in for it, 'cause 'e sent 'is Son to take the chop instead of us?"

"'Wouldn't quite put it jus' like that," Eddie replied, "But, yes, I think you've got it".

"'That ain't fair," said Private Robbie Petrie. "That tale just makes me downright angry."

'But I 'ave to tell you, Reverend, them squaddies went very quiet. It was like a big strong hand 'ad taken hold of us. We couldn't even 'ear the guns no more, an if I 'adn't seen it wi' my own eyes, I wouldn't 've believed it. Jack Pidley sat there sobbin' like a baby. 'E jus' kept sayin', "'elp me, 'elp me!" We was all listenin' when Jack spoke up. 'E was some'ow different, confident an' calm, an e spoke again.

"'If anyone wants to pray with me, remember God's waitin' an listenin' an' you'll never pray a more important prayer as long as you live. We're goin' to say thanks to 'im for sendin' 'is only Son to take away all our sins, an' we're goin' to ask 'im to give us a clean new heart an' a new life.'"

The Reverend Ambrose Muir bowed his head and clasped his hands. As an eager young vicar, he had responded to his calling like a man who believed his chosen life was God's gift to him and he had been determined to serve with all his heart. But as the years passed, and as decades of disappointing and frustrating ministry had quenched the fire which had all but died, his soul had succumbed to the tedium of what had become a repetitive ritual. His congregation had diminished to a few faithful adherents, a handful of whom he may well outlive only to perform that last solemn service as one by one they would fall prey to the last enemy.

The loss of his gallant son and his beloved wife had left him with a smouldering resentment in his heart against the God whom he'd tried his best to serve. And now here, in this dim room, sitting opposite him at the stained oak tea table, was a young, naive Lance Corporal who'd related a living spiritual experience which had struck a forgotten chord deep in his soul.

'Private Eddie Watts prayed that prayer,' Aaron went on, 'an' 'e told us we could pray the words after 'im, out loud if we wanted, but if we was shy, we could just say it to ourselves, 'cause God would 'ear it anyway. It were all strange to me, vicar, but I found myself prayin' inside, sayin' what Eddie was sayin, an' the funny thing is, Reverend, I was really meanin' it. There was no way o' knowin' if anyone else joined in, except that Jack Pidley prayed out loud. That's what surprised us all.

'After 'e said the 'amen,' 'e threw 'is arms around Eddie 'an 'e were laughin' an' talkin' an' cryin' all at once. Then 'e rubbed 'is face an' 'is chest with 'is 'ands an' kept sayin' 'e was new an' clean, an' to tell the truth, Reverend, I felt a bubblin' deep inside an' I wanted to give Jack a hug 'cause at that minute I 'ad a feelin' of love for 'im in my heart like I'd never known before.

'When I asked Eddie what 'ad 'appened to us, 'e said the Holy Spirit 'ad come into our hearts and Jesus was livin' in us now. 'E gave Jack the little Testament 'cause 'e'd thrown 'is away an' 'e put it in the breast pocket of 'is tunic. I looked through my kit an' found mine, an' there it is,  Reverend, on this very table. No-one in that fox 'ole said a word. It were jus' like they'd all been struck dumb.'

The Reverend Ambrose Muir sat in silence; his head bowed. The lamplight picked out a scattering of brown freckles, showing through his sparse grey hair. His shoulders shook a little as one by one a tear fell on the dull table-top, leaving a dark stain.

'Lord Jesus Christ, have mercy', he said, 'Have mercy on me'.

Lance Corporal Fleming felt the vicar's pain in his own heart and he hesitantly reached out and laid his hand on the hand of the grieving clergyman. But the story wasn't finished.

Chapter Three

Aaron continued. 'Next mornin' at six we were lined up in the trenches,' he said. He stopped, interrupting himself. 'Shall I go on, Reverend?' The vicar nodded without looking up.

'You're the only one I can talk with. You were closer to my son Craig at the end than anyone else I know. I want to hear about the battle.'

'So as I was sayin',' Aaron went on, 'There we were, all lined up in the trenches, thousands of us, waiting for the whistle, like footballers, all tensed up waiting for a match to start.

'Suddenly Private Robbie Petrie, of all people, started prayin', "Our Father which art in heaven, hallowed be Thy name". One by one we all joined in. "Thy kingdom come, Thy will be done on earth..."

'The whistle blew an' startled us. We weren't ready but there was no 'oldin' back. We scrambled up the trench ladders an' over the top we went. Some of us didn't get but fifteen yards. The young officer commandin' our platoon was cut down right next to me. All around us men was fallin'; some was wounded an' went crawlin' on, groanin' an' screamin'. Funny thing was, Reverend, I wasn't scared. We was only yards from the enemy trenches when Eddie Watts fell. 'E were crumpled up on all fours, face in the mud. I saw Jack Pidley crouch over 'im. 'E hoisted Eddie up to 'is feet, pushed 'is shoulder under 'im an' set off back to our trenches. 'E 'adn't gone but ten paces when 'e was hit as well. 'E spun round an' was hit again. 'E were knocked off 'is balance an' lay there wi' Eddie on top of 'im.

'We took the enemy trench that day, but thousands fell, killed an' wounded. Shouldn't be surprised, Reverend, if Lieutenant Muir was lost in that dreadful battle. Next mornin' the stretcher bearers went out to carry in the wounded. They brought Eddie's body in, shot through the heart, he was, but Jack Pidley was alive. 'E'd laid all night under Eddie. Couldn't move 'cause 'is left leg was shattered above 'is knee. The field surgeon was lookin' 'im over, preparin' to amputate the leg when 'e noticed a bullet 'ole in the breast pocket 'o 'is tunic. He looks at the nurse an' says, "This soldier was shot twice." 'E undoes Jack's pocket an' takes out Eddie's testament. There was a shell embedded in it. Jack thought to treasure and keep the Testament, but after some consideration he sent it to Eddie's mother wi' the whole account o' what happened.'

* * *

The two men sat in silence for a few moments. Aaron cleared his throat.

'I was meanin' to ask you, Reverend, if you, bein' a man of God, as it were, might say a prayer for me. You see, I keep seein' things, awful things, mostly at night, but anything'll set 'em off, things I saw done and things what I done myself. It's not a peaceful life for me now, Vicar, an' I was wonderin' if you might ask the Holy Spirit to drive the fears and the visions away. I've been readin' this Testament an' I can see these visions ain't comin'' from Jesus.'

The Reverend Ambrose Muir responded like a man transformed. He sat upright in his chair, reached out and took up the little book. Leafing through the pages, he quickly found the passage he was looking for.

'Romans chapter 8, verses 35 to 39,' he announced in a voice which at once both claimed Aaron's attention and sent a thrill to his heart.

'Who shall separate us from the love of Christ? Shall tribulation, or distress, or persecution, or famine, or nakedness or peril, or sword? As it is written, For thy sake we are killed all the day long; we are accounted as sheep for the slaughter. Nay, in all these things we are more than conquerors through him that loved us. For I am persuaded that neither death, nor life, nor angels, nor principalities, nor powers, nor things present, nor things to come, nor height, nor depth, nor any other creature, shall be able to separate us from the love of God, which is in Christ Jesus our Lord.' (AV)

Epilogue

Aaron was trembling with a sense of overwhelming love. The vicar's reading had brought so vividly to mind those hideous scenes which had haunted him day and night since the war's end and yet shining above all was the glory of the cross of Jesus.

"If you want to know how much God loves you," Eddie had said to Private Pidley the blasphemer, "look at the cross."

Both men bowed their heads.

'Thank you, Father in heaven,' the Reverend began, 'thank you for sending my young friend Aaron to minister to us this afternoon. We have both suffered much, more than we are able to bear, so that our spirit has been brought to places which are so dark that we are blinded to your love. Renew us again, our Father, by the grace and power of your Spirit and revive that which is dying in us, through Jesus Christ our Lord, who loves us and who gave himself for us, Amen.'

Aaron felt again that joy welling up within him which he had known in the trenches. As the two men stood up, they inadvertently embraced each other.

'A new beginning' the vicar said. 'May the grace of our Lord Jesus Christ, and the love of God, and the fellowship of the Holy Spirit, be with us and remain with us, now and for evermore.'

The Shipwreck

Introduction

Two men abandoned a stricken ship in a violent storm, as the vessel sank with all other hands and passengers lost. One of the survivors, Midshipman Plummett, was hurled into the raging seas clutching a leather pouch which held twenty-seven gold guineas which had fallen from the coat pocket of a wealthy merchant as he was swept overboard. His shipmate, Master Crabbe, one of the ship's cooks, had seized hold of a wooden box which had floated up from the galley; it contained a loaf of bread, a large cheese and a bottle of fresh water.

The stout box had helped him to stay afloat. Aided by strong currents, the two survivors found themselves washed up on a small island, a small outcrop of volcanic rock; it was stark and bare without tree, plant or any form of shelter.

Neither of the castaways seemed willing to reveal what each had saved from the shipwreck, but grateful for their survival and exhausted by their efforts, they fell into a fitful sleep. As the hours of darkness passed first one, and then the other would stir, the one checking his inside pocket to ensure that the leather pouch had not been discovered by his fellow survivor, while his companion would waken with a start and tighten his grip on his precious box, which he held to his breast like a sleeping child.

Chapter One

The day after the shipwreck dawned fair and bright. The ship was gone, swallowed up by the ocean which stretched away—calm, vast and empty into the horizon. Watched closely by his companion, Master Crabbe opened the wooden box, tore a little bread from the loaf and broke away a small piece of cheese. Taking a sip from the water bottle, he ate the bread and cheese, chewing slowly, his eyes half closed. He sighed, with a little grunt like a man who had just  enjoyed a hearty meal, replaced the stopper on the bottle and carefully packed it away with the bread and cheese.

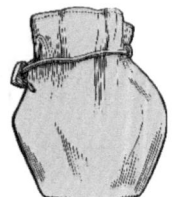 Unable to resist a comparison with the worth of his own plunder, the Midshipman drew the pouch from his inside pocket and tapped it gently. The coins made that unmistakable chinking sound when gold guineas are shaken together.

Master Crabbe's ears twitched at the sound. 'Music,' said Midshipman Plummett, the beneficiary of the merchant's misfortune. 'Ain't no tune on earth compares with the clink o'gold!' He removed one of the coins and held it up to the sunlight, turning it so that it flashed and glittered.

'Got more'n two dozen o' them little beauties,' he claimed. 'Now if you were to share me 'alf your water 'n bread 'n cheese, I might just see my way to let you 'ave one o' these 'ere guineas.'

'Now there's a bargain,' answered his shipmate. 'If we was safe ashore I'd give it serious consideration, but seein' as how we've been left out here, between sea an' sky an' no sign o' rescue, I reckon as how my bread 'n cheese an' water's worth more to me even than one o' your gold guineas!'

With that, Master Crabbe stretched himself, gave an irritating burp, and pretended to nod off. But there was no real rest for him, and he was left wondering how he would fare if his companion attacked him. He tensed his muscles, as though preparing for hand-to-hand combat, watching his fellow castaway through half-closed eyes.

The sun rose until it seemed directly above the little island, staring down like a burning eye. Crabbe opened his picnic box and took out the bread, cheese and the water bottle.

'Just a little bite to keep the strength up,' he explained. His companion stared at him with a malevolent glare, as Crabbe again made a small rough sandwich for himself. Looking upward, he held the bread and cheese aloft. With half-closed eyes he said sanctimoniously, 'For what I'm just about to receive, may I be truly thankful.' He chewed the dry bread thoughtfully. 'Jus' wash it down now.' He allowed himself as little water as he dared. 'Got about enough to last me three days if I'm very careful,' he said. 'Who knows, a ship might come by.'

'That's right, that's right,' said Plummett, wiping perspiration from his brow and licking his dry lips. 'Sure to be a ship! Merchantmen pass this way regular. Oh there'll be a ship alright. But 'til one comes, we could do a little business! I've bin thinkin'. I'm ready to share an' share alike, like two honest shipmates, 'alf 'n 'alf! 'alf my guineas for 'alf your vittles! Can't say fairer! An' when a ship comes sailin' along, we'll be rich an' appy shipmates!'

'Rich?' said Master Crabbe, the custodian of the bread, cheese and priceless water. 'Even if we're dead 'n found like two fish, dried in the sun 'n a ship comes, 'n finds us too late, who'll be rich then? You done a wrong thing, robbin' that gold, Midshipman!'

As the day dragged on, Midshipman Plummett's discomfort intensified. Gnawing hunger and raging thirst reduced him to such a state of weakness that in spite of the pitiless heat he began to shudder, as though suffering from bitter cold. His teeth chattered and he would now and again call out, like a man in dread of some threatening presence. In his hallucinations he saw the drifting ghosts of lost shipmates. He saw the merchant, whose treasure he had looted, his face bloated, eyes colourless and bulging, hands reaching out as though to drag the Midshipman down into that dreadful place. Master Crabbe watched in silence. 'The end will come soon,' he thought, 'And then all will be mine.'

Chapter Two

At length the sun began its descent into the sea on the western horizon. The air cooled rapidly bringing relief to Master Crabbe. To his astonishment, the Midshipman stirred and slowly sat up, looking around like a man who had awakened from a dream. A cool moist wind blew in from the sea and as the two castaways watched, a heavy cloud piled up out of the west and rolled across the evening sky. Midshipman Plummett, who had suffered a day of such intolerable thirst that he had stared into the faces of the dead, croaked with excitement as the blessed cloud began to scatter sweet fat drops of rain on the rocky island.

As the rain intensified, he scooped the refreshing gift of water from the rock pools and rolled to and fro' on the damp stone as his clothing absorbed the precious moisture. He clasped his hands together in an attitude of prayer and called out with a voice pregnant with emotion, 'Thank'ee, thank'ee God up there in 'eaven, for such a merciful gift!'

His adversary—for that is what Crabbe had become—was infuriated by the Midshipman's relief, and his irritating devotions. He cursed the rain, which was now a tropical downpour. Growling like a disgruntled bear, he crouched over his sandwich box, determined to keep his treasure dry, while at the same time trying to spread his coat around his shivering person. Each time he moved a fresh trickle of water ran down the back of his neck.

'Damn this filthy rain!' he muttered loudly, even as Midshipman Plummett lay on his back, arms outstretched, mouth wide open, luxuriating in blessed relief.

As a new day dawned, however, a warm west wind chased the cloud across the sky. It scattered into ragged fragments which faded into the sunrise.

'There'll be a ship, today,' said the Midshipman, trying to sound confident.

'What makes you say such a thing?' asked the other.

'Stands to reason,' came the answer.

'Reason, what reason? Jus' look out there! What d'ye see? The emptiest sight o' nothin' in this world! Me, I'm a bit peckish. Reckon it's breakfast time!' And the pitiless custodian of foodstuffs, eager to press home his unmerciful advantage, once again allowed himself a rough little bread and cheese sandwich, followed by a disciplined swig from his water bottle.

'Reckon we're in for a real scorcher,' he said as he packed away his provisions. 'Bread,' he said simply. He held up what remained of his precious loaf, as though preparing to address an imaginary audience. 'Bread,' he said again emphatically. 'Staff o' life! That's what they call it, them as know; I'm talkin' about this 'ere bread! Staff o' life. That's what's kept in that there box.

Them guineas o' yours, root of all evil, they are! That's what the good book says!'

* * *

Midshipman Plummett, once again feeling the threatening heat of the sun, trembled with hunger; the brief respite he had enjoyed from the night's rain had passed and already his throat was parched and dry so that his breath came in hot rasping gasps. He could not deny his companion's devastating reasoning. His horde of gold had not only lost its allure, but it also now seemed to hang upon him like the curse of judgement. All he could do was make one last effort to preserve his life for one more day. Too weak now to contemplate attacking his fellow castaway, he would resort to appealing to that condition of human weakness to which he reckoned all men are, in the end, susceptible—the allure of gold. He began his appeal by using the ploy of flattery.

'What you said about the staff o' life,' he said. 'I never knowed you was such a scholar. If I was half as wise as you, I wouldn't be in this fix. I would've done what you done an' made sure I had somethin' to keep us alive 'til a ship came by. Then we could've shared what we 'ad like two honest shipmates that survived the storm together.'

He ran the tip of his tongue over his cracked lips. Then, withdrawing the pouch of coins from his pocket he poured them out slowly on to a rock. In spite of himself, his companion seemed unable to resist looking out of the corner of one eye at the glistening little pile of pure gold.

'Just one proper sized bit o' bread with a bit o' cheese an' a good swig o' water an' twenty o' them guineas is yours,' said the Midshipman.

'How many o' them guineas 'ave you got, then?' asked the sandwich man.

'Twenty-seven,' came the answer. There was a short silence.

'I want the lot then,' said Master Crabbe, 'All of 'em.' Midshipman Plummett sensed a deal might at last be possible.

'Can't do it,' he said. 'May as well jus' hang on an' take my chances.'

'Up to you,' was the reply. 'All or nothin', them's my terms!'

Despite the heat, the midshipman began to shiver or rather shudder. He felt that he was perhaps once again close to that dreaded end which all men must face. The small heap of gold at his side seemed like a divine judgement. He'd heard it called filthy lucre many a time. Would he not be in a better state to be rid of it?

'If we shake on it, it's a deal, then?' he asked.

'It's a deal,' said the other.

'But hold on a minute! Not so fast my good friend,' interjected Plummett. 'You can see them guineas there, plain as day. Show me how much bread an' cheese I'm gettin', an' how much water.'

As the Midshipman began to shuffle towards his shipmate in order to ensure he wouldn't be short changed, he saw over his shoulder, out to the southwest, a sight which stopped his heart for an instant. He tried to speak, but no sound came out of his mouth, which opened and closed as silently as the mouth of a beached cod.

Meanwhile his companion had removed the bread, cheese and water bottle and was marking off a slice of bread with his thumbnail. Midshipman Plummett gave him a sharp shove, so that he lost his balance. Thinking that his treasured food store was in danger of being plundered he threw it all back in the box and spread-eagled himself upon it.

'Deal's off! Deal's off!' he yelled angrily. But suddenly the Midshipman found his voice. His fatigue and weakness seemed to miraculously vanish.

'Ship!' he shouted. 'It's a ship! God's 'eard my prayers! He's sent a ship to save me!' He crouched down in an attitude of prayer over his treasure and gathered the guineas, counting them one by one as he carefully returned them to the pouch.

'I'm rich,' he muttered. 'Thank you God, I'm rich!' Master Crabbe scanned the horizon.

'No ship out there,' he said sullenly. But Midshipman Plummett was having none of it.

'Have you gone stone blind,' he demanded. 'Southwest, man, southwest!'

It was true! There on the horizon was a large vessel which appeared to be on a course that might easily pass the tiny island.

'We 'ad a deal,' said Master Crabbe, 'a gentleman's agreement but you soon tidied away them guineas. They're mine by rights.' The Midshipman, who seemed to have found a new source of energy, snorted with derisive laughter.

'You've gone mad,' he roared. 'You can keep yer mouldy bread'n cheese. That vessel's on its way! It'll be ship's grog 'n vittles for me in no time! Look! Look! 'ere she comes, God bless 'er!'

He took two guineas from his pocket and held them up to the sun. They flashed brilliantly as he turned them in the sunlight.

'They've seen us,' the Midshipman yelled. Master Crabbe opened his box and approached Midshipman Plummett.

''Alf 'n 'alf, you said, like two honest shipmates, we'll both be rich. Them's your very own words!'

The Midshipman dashed the box to the ground. The ship had lowered a boat and four of the crew were rowing steadily towards them. He kicked the sandwich box into the sea.

'No, no, no!' screamed Master Crabbe hysterically. 'Just an hour gone the price o' that bread, cheese 'n water was seven an' twenty guineas!'

Chapter Three

As the rowers arrived the castaways scrambled into the boat. The rowers put about and began pulling strongly towards their ship.

'We was shipwrecked,' said Midshipman Plummett breathlessly.

'Aye,' said one of the rescue crew. 'We 'eard there was a lively storm wi' all hands lost. We saw your signal flashin' like a beacon. T'were like a miracle an' no mistake!'

'It was 'im what did that,' said Master Crabbe with a treacherous glint in his eye. 'He used two o' them bright gold guineas what 'e took from a drownin' merchant when our ship was lost. 'E's got twenty seven of 'em in a purse in 'is pocket.'

'Well, well, well, now,' said the spokesman of the rescue party 'Well, well, well! To think we're jus' four poor an' simple God-fearin' seamen. An', as such we've an honest interest in seein' justice done. We wouldn't wish the theft o' treasure from an 'elpless drownin' man to be tormentin' yer consciences.' He drew a pistol from his belt, cocked it and aimed straight at Midshipman Plummett.

'Up on yer feet,' he ordered, 'An' empty yer pockets.' The Midshipman rose unsteadily, his head swimming. He had been cast into the teeth of a furious storm, suffered the torments of hell itself and stared into the ghastly face of death. He would not surrender his treasure to these thieves!

In his mind's eye he saw again the stricken ship. He saw the merchant, clinging desperately to the rail of the doomed vessel. He saw the thunderous wave which spun the merchant round, and the heavy pouch which flew from the pocket of his greatcoat. He saw the merchant fall to his hands and knees, reaching out in desperation for his lost treasure, and he saw the great wave which rolled the prostrate merchant over and over until it bore him away into the darkness of the storm. As the Midshipman was swept across the deck he had reached out and seized the doomed merchant's gold guineas which had almost cost him his life.

Midshipman Plummett lurched towards the threatening sailor. His eyes were glazed and fixed upon nothing. The very one who had rowed out to rescue the castaways squeezed the trigger. The Midshipman's arms flailed wildly, the rescue boat lurched sharply and Midshipman Plummett was thrown overboard. His coat floated out like a pair of wings as he lay face down, unmoving in the water. The heavy leather pouch slid from his pocket and sank like a stone into the depths of the dark water.

'Get 'im, get 'im,' screamed Master Crabbe as the body of his shipmate floated away. After some adept work at the oars

Midshipman Plummett's lifeless body was hauled into the rescue boat. The crew fell upon the dead man like vultures on a corpse. They ransacked his pockets, tore out the linings and left him looking like a man who had been savaged by wild animals. They turned their attention to Master Crabbe.

'What was all that talk o' gold guineas?' demanded one. The menace in his voice unnerved Master Crabbe.

'Must've slipped from 'is coat pocket in the water.' His voice trembled with anxiety.

'Well I'm thinkin' it may just be that you're the one what's concealin' somethin' from us.'

'No! No!' said Master Crabbe earnestly, 'I'm just an able seaman, a ship's cook, I'm nobody! Where would I find gold guineas, out there shipwrecked on an island!' His tormentor drew a wicked looking blade from its sheath.

'Better 'ave a look then didn't we?' he said threateningly, 'bein' as you're the one what mentioned drownin' merchants an' stolen treasure!'

Master Crabbe stood to his feet, took off his coat. laid it down and turned the pockets of his breeches inside out. He held out empty hands beseechingly. He heard a commotion and looked back towards the island. A flock of yelping seabirds was squabbling over the last remains of his precious loaf of bread.

'Throw 'im overboard,' the spokesman said callously, 'Send 'im back where 'e come from. 'E ain't no use to us!'

Relieved to be alive, Master Crabbe struck out strongly towards the island. Kindly currents swept him along. As he approached the rocky refuge, he saw something bobbing ahead. It was his water bottle, still half full. 'Perhaps it'll rain tonight,' he thought. 'Perhaps a proper rescue ship'll come by tomorrow.' As he clambered ashore, the four seamen boarded their ship. The captain ordered the ship's flag to be run up. The skull and crossbones fluttered overhead in the fading evening light.

Epilogue

'Do not be deceived, my beloved brothers. Every good gift and every perfect gift is from above, coming down from the Father of lights, with whom there is no variation or shadow due to change. Of his own will he brought us forth by the word of truth, that we should be a kind of first-fruits of his creatures.' James 1:16-18 (ESV)

James B. Duffy

Introduction

A motley handful of protestors had gathered in front of a small stone cottage which had stood on the summit of a gently rising hillock for more than three hundred years about a mile outside the tiny village of Brixtock. The lane which wound its way up the rise to the cottage was really a cart track, bordered with broom and gorse, which thinned out as it reached the house, leaving a surrounding meadow of wild flowers and grassland which Nelly Crowther, the farmer's wife, had named Larks' Drift. It stretched away over the hillock and beyond, sweeping down a long, wide hill into a valley where a row of trees followed the stream which fed Shelley's pool, before winding its way through the landscape like an ancient artery until it vanished among the rolling contours of the farmland. Down at the junction, just a hundred yards from the cottage where the lane left the main road, a large piece of ground had been cleared. A green portacabin stood amongst a small number of yellow earth-moving monsters and diggers which sat silently in the mud, awaiting the signal to charge at the defenceless landscape and leave it wounded and scarred forever.

'What, we must ask ourselves, is at stake here,' said the rather formidable woman whose authoritative bearing had presumed unopposed leadership of the protestors. 'This proposed bypass is nothing less than wanton desecration of an area of outstanding natural beauty, to say nothing of the destruction of an important natural resource which is the ancient breeding ground of toads, frogs and newts. Of equal importance in some ways, is the humanitarian aspect of this whole tragic business. Poor Mr Duffy, an octogenarian, a veteran and a war hero, who was actually physically born here in Skein Cottage, is shortly to be evicted, in order to make way for this wretched road, for which, an independent study has concluded, there is no urgent necessity!'

There was a ragged chorus of 'Hear, hear!' from the group which brought a look of satisfied approval from the spokesperson. She was certainly a commanding figure of a woman, blessed with a copious bosom, a broad face with thin lips, outlined with very dark red lipstick and immaculately waved iron grey hair. Unlike the rest of the group, most of whom were dressed in casual hooded jackets and either joggers or torn jeans, she wore a smart tweed skirt suit, green woollen stockings and leather ankle boots. A large canvas satchel hung over her left shoulder containing suitable rainwear in the event of inclement weather and in her right hand she held a polished blackthorn walking stick.

Chapter One

Dennis (Sniffer) Shaw braked as he approached the earthmovers and the portacabin.

'That's the place,' he said to his passenger. He peered up the lane. 'Ah well, better go and have a look,' he said, 'after all there's nothing much else going on.' He bumped his way up the dirt track and climbed out of his car. 'Bring the camera,' he called to his companion. 'Might as well make the most of it while we're here.' He drew a notebook from an inside pocket and approached the protestors.

'Blimey, we've got a right lot here,' he muttered under his breath. 'Right,' he said briskly, 'So who's in charge here?' Dennis had more than twenty years of experience in the art of sniffing out stories and he homed straight in on the spokesperson. 'Good afternoon, madam. I understand that this is a protest against the new bypass. I'd be obliged if you gave me your point of view and I'm sure my readers would like to know your name.' She sniffed and looked around at her little flock.

'I'm sure nobody would be the slightest bit interested in my name. We're all together in this. However, I'm not ashamed of this protest, and if you really think that knowing my name would serve to arouse awareness of what is proposed here, I'll tell you who I am. My name, sir, is Edith Sproston." She drew back her shoulders and tossed her head very slightly as she divulged her identity. There was a sympathetic ripple of approval from the protestors, some of whom hoisted up their banners as though to emphasise their commitment to the mission.

'Can we have a picture, Edith?' asked the reporter.

'If you photograph us all,' she answered, 'with our placards.' She turned to the brave little group of eco warriors. 'This gentleman is Mr ?' She nodded to Dennis.

'Shaw,' he said, 'Reporter of local news for the Echo, and this is Russ Norris, our press photographer. We're doing an article for tomorrow's edition. We need to sort it out, all neat and tidy, A.S.A.P.' The protestors huddled together. Two or three thrust their placards forward aggressively, obscuring their faces. 'NO! NO! NO!' said one, the bright red paint dribbling from the lettering as though it was bleeding. 'NO WAY! NO WAY!' said another. The artist had misjudged her lettering and had run out of space so that the last three letters and the exclamation mark were crushed together like sardines. The photographer focused his camera.

'Come on now, don't be shy! Hold those placards high and let's see your faces!' A young woman dressed in a combat jacket with an enormous hood which enveloped most of her face shuffled her way out of the group and stood aside, a few yards away. She had called in sick that morning and had offered her trusty 'migraine' excuse to her sceptical employer whose patience, she knew, was pretty well exhausted; as a single parent, she desperately needed to keep her job and the very last thing she wanted was her photograph in the paper. Jack took a few photographs and turned to Dennis.

'We finished here then?' he asked.

'No, don't put your gear away yet. We're only half done,' he answered. He turned to Ms Sproston.

'So what d'you know about the old man? Duffy, isn't it? Have you spoken to him yet? I'd need a picture of him. After all, isn't this what it's all about, him being kicked out of his house?'

Ms Sproston looked apprehensive. She raised her eyebrows and pulled her lips down at the corners. She sucked in almost a lungful of breath before blowing it out with puffed cheeks.

'You've hit on a rather touchy issue, Mr Shaw,' she said in a conspiratorial voice, glancing at her supporters. 'You see we have been strongly advised not to contact Mr Duffy on any pretext whatsoever. Naturally he is extremely upset about this whole unfortunate business. I understand that he is an octogenarian and that he is so entrenched in his way of life here in Skein Cottage that he is inclined to dangerous rages when approached on the subject of moving on. In addition to this, it's feared that he may be armed!'

Edith Sproston's revelation was a powerful stimulus to Dennis Shaw. Here was a situation which he could develop into a seriously provocative story. If he could persuade old Duffy to give him an interview and pose for a photograph he might just have a pretty good day after all.

'Come on Russ, keep right behind me,' the intrepid reporter urged as he approached Skein Cottage. Heavy chenille curtains covered the downstairs windows. There was no fenced garden so that the front door opened to natural grass. It was as though the whole landscape beyond belonged to the old stone house. Dennis lifted the heavy cast iron door knocker and gave three loud raps. He waited for a moment with an ear cocked, listening for some response from within. He turned to Russ.

'Not a whisper,' he muttered. 'What d'you reckon?' Russ shrugged.

'Try calling through the letter box,' he suggested. Dennis pushed the flap aside,

'Hello,' he roared. 'It's Dennis Shaw, reporter for the Echo! We want to write a story about the way you've been treated. We want to help you! Can you open up so we can have a chat?'

The two men looked up as they heard the sound of a first floor sash window opening. A shot gun barrel appeared, followed by an angry face. Jacob B. Duffy wriggled his shoulders through the open window and pushed upwards so that half his upper body was free to aim the shotgun. He pointed it at the two men who stood open-mouthed, staring up at him.

'Get a shot, Russ! Get a photograph,' said Dennis urgently.

'You two vermin, you got ten seconds to get off my property!' Jacob cocked the hammers for each barrel and pulled the gunstock into his shoulder. 'You've 'ad five, just five more,' said Jacob B. Duffy. He started counting, 'One, two three,' he said menacingly as the intrepid newsmen turned and ran for their lives. He closed the window and the house again fell silent. As they returned to the protest group

Dennis said excitedly, 'That's it then! That's just absolutely it! Got to get a move on. It'll be in the paper tomorrow!' They climbed into the car and went bumping away as quickly as the cart track would allow. 'You did get a shot, Russ,' the reporter asked his companion.

'Yeah, at least one cracking shot,' Russ assured him.

'Thank heaven for that! I'd hate to think we'd risked our lives for nothing!' he replied. 'Never saw such a tough-looking old geezer, did you?'

Chapter Two

Jacob Duffy stood with his wife at the rear of Skein Cottage. They had just locked the chickens away for the night and checked the ferrets' cage. A sharp looking Jack Russell terrier sat at their feet staring up at them. They had been married for more than twenty years, yet each evening they would try to join one another in the last chores of the day. They had married in 1946 after Jacob had left the army following the cessation of hostilities and had remained devoted to one another.

Hannah was a slim, shy girl who had worked on the farm as a land girl during the final year of the war. She had been brought up in an orphanage, and there was a vulnerability about her which Jacob, a straightforward, powerfully built countryman found irresistible. She had grey, thoughtful eyes and sun-bleached hair which fell in natural waves to her shoulders. Jacob, who was almost eight years older than the guileless, graceful Hannah, was instantly smitten and although she sometimes made him feel clumsy and awkward, he had dared to propose to her just three months after they had met.

'I thought you were going to ask me,' she said shyly, 'and I already decided I'd say yes.'

After a short engagement, they were married in the parish church. They lived together with Jacob's parents in Skein Cottage where he had been born. Tragedy had struck the family just before his fortieth birthday when Jacob's mother had collapsed with a crushing stroke from which she never recovered. His father was so devastated by the sudden passing of his wife that he seemed to lose all interest in anything but the secret world he shared with the memory of the wife he had lost He would sit on the old oak bench outside the back door of the house and sing in a gentle voice until after dark. The tunes would be familiar, but he would mumble his own words, secret confidences which nobody else could share. He would hardly eat and lost so much weight that when he caught pneumonia one winter he told the village doctor that he had no fight left in him. He said that the doctor wasn't to worry because he didn't intend to live any longer, and he just drifted away.

One late autumn evening, as Jacob and Hannah sat outside watching the sun going down, a flight of twenty or thirty rooks passed overhead.

'They're flyin' 'ome,' Jacob told her. 'They're goin' to their roostin' place to settle down for the night, side by side.'

One of the birds had fallen behind and was calling, just like a tired child. It's partner peeled away from the rest and turned back, flying in a large circle and calling out until it had joined the weary straggler. The two of them flew on together.

'That's you an' me,' Hannah said, reaching out and taking his hand. 'Sometimes I'll need you to 'elp me an' sometimes I'll need to 'elp you.'

'You can tell when rooks is flyin' 'ome, Jacob told her solemnly. 'They always fly west, into the settin' sun. Don't exactly know why, but it's a fact.'

Chapter Three

One summer evening, Charlie Crowther, the farmer who was Jacob's employer, arrived at Skein Cottage in a battered old Land Rover. The driver's door opened and the old man lifted his right leg with both hands and planted his foot on the ground. Leaning on a stout stick held in his right hand he dragged his left leg out of the cab, reached back with his left hand for another stick and heaved himself out of the old jalopy, tottering forward as he almost lost his balance.

Hannah hurried from the house, calling out, 'No, Charlie, No! Let me 'elp you. Please, Charlie, will you just…' Farmer Crowther waved her away.

'I can manage, I'm not an invalid,' he said as he crouched over his walking sticks. 'Go inside an' put on the kettle. I'll be with you in a minute or two.' Hannah stared at him and shook her head.

'Men!' she said, 'What can you do with them!'

Ten minutes later, Charlie Crowther, Jacob and Hannah were sitting on the bench which stood against the wall outside the back door holding mugs of tea.

'I've come to talk a little business talk,' Charlie began. 'Thing is, I'm not what I used to be. The farm's too much for me now; you get tired, you know. Ain't got no family 'cept my sister, an' that Milly Hargreaves what's been doin' for me with the washin' an' cookin'. She's not up to it no more, an' I don't want all the trouble of lookin' elsewhere, so I'm sellin' the farm an' goin' to put up with my sister.' There was a short, stunned silence. Hannah took Jacob's hand and squeezed it tightly.

'But I want you to know that I've made arrangements,' Charlie went on. 'I ain't forgotten that your father worked for my father an' that you were born 'ere in this cottage, an' you've worked for nobody else, only me, 'ceptin' them army days. The farm's goin' to one o' them big conglomerates, I think they're called. They might take you on, Jacob, and they might not. They wouldn't promise, but I couldn't 'ave you put out of your 'ouse. I just couldn't. Your father'd haunt me if I did such a thing, so I've 'ad a document drawn up, all legal an' tidy an' all signed up, givin' you the tenancy o' Skein Cottage, rent free, 'til your dyin' day, an' should you pass on before Hannah, she's covered as well. You're to get your own personal copy o' the agreement, so look after it.'

Jacob rested his hand on Charlie Crowther's shoulder. He could feel the old man's bones through his threadbare jacket.

'I always wondered when this day would come, Charlie,' he said quietly. 'Fact is, when I thought about it, it scared me, but you've done us proud, Charlie, an' God should bless you, 'cause if anyone deserves God's blessin', it's you.'

* * *

Shortly after Charlie Crowther moved away, the new manager of Cray Valley farm paid Jacob a visit. He arrived in an almost new Range Rover and, after looking in appraisal for some time at Skein Cottage knocked confidently at the door. He was smartly dressed in the young countryman's style with a nicely cut tweed suit and brogue shoes. He wore his old college tie, and Jacob thought that he spoke in a rather cultured voice. He seemed to be about thirty years old.

'So, here we are,' he said briskly as the three stood together in the living room. 'Nice to meet you. My name is Jeremy Melville.' They all shook hands. 'I understand that you were born in this house, Mr Duffy,' he began. 'Built in 1690? The house, I mean, not you! Ha,ha,ha! Looks as though it could do with some renovation, the house, I mean,' he said again, with another irritating laugh. 'Well, it's yours, at least for the time being; we won't be getting our hands on it 'til you're gone. Old man Crowther made sure of that.

'This is simply a courtesy call, but while I'm here, we may as well straighten out a few issues. Crowther said that you'd be willing to do some work for us, and indeed he recommended you very highly as a reliable worker. However, it's only fair to point out that there will be a lot of changes here. The whole enterprise is seriously in need of modernisation and we'll be doing things differently. Consequently, we have our own staff, people who are trained and qualified to optimise output and efficiency. It may well be that we might wish to call on you from time to time as a casual labourer. Indeed, this could well be reasonably frequent, but we cannot offer hope of permanent employment.' Jacob nodded.

'I understand, Mr Melville,' he said politely. 'Would you like tea?'

'No, no! needs must, but thanks anyway. It's been good to meet you.'

He shook Jacob's hand, turned to Hannah and inclined his head politely. Then he turned and was gone.

Chapter Four

Within a year Jacob and Hannah attended Charlie Crowther's funeral. He was brought home to be buried in the Parish Church graveyard to comply with his wishes. Hannah choked with emotion as they said their farewells to the old man.

'Don't know why that old hymn got to me like that,' she said apologetically. 'Abide with me, I mean. "Help of the helpless, O abide with me," it says. Come to think about it, when it comes to dyin' we're all 'elpless, every one of us. D'you think there's anything in it, Jacob? In religion, I mean, 'cause if God isn't the 'elp of the 'elpless, why 'ave I got this lump 'ere?' She placed her hand on her heart.

'Best not think about it too much,' Jacob answered. 'It'll pass. Best not to dwell on them things; they can get you into trouble. That's 'ow I got my nose broke!'

Hannah looked up at him and ran her forefinger down his profile.

'Tin't straight,' she giggled, 'But I do like it. Makes you look like you can look after us. You've always said you got into a fight, but you've never said why. Was it over a girl?'

He shook his head. ''Ow many times 'ave I told you. You was the first, an' you'll be the last. Ain't nobody else for me, never was, never will be.'

As he spoke, she took a strand of her hair and curled it round her finger, looking up into his face.

'Alright, I'll tell you what 'appened,' he said, 'so you can stop guessin'. When we was called up we was posted to a basic training camp. That's where they tried to knock us into shape. I was fit an' strong 'cause I'd been workin' on the farm since I was fourteen, but some of us weren't cut out for runnin' up hills an' woods an' crawlin' through 'eavy mud wi' an eighty pound pack on our backs so some of them got rough treatment.

'There was one lad, Herbert Biddles, 'e was called who came from Norfolk. 'E were a country lad, like me, but 'e wasn't very strong. We used to talk together 'cause 'e was interested in birds an' wild animals. 'E 'ad a notebook with a lot o' drawin's 'e'd done. Marvellous, they were, 'E could draw any bird, just from memory. 'E said it were a gift from God who'd made everything on the whole earth an' given us eyes to see what 'e's like. 'E were harmless, really, but 'e upset some of us, sayin' what 'e did. 'Ed been a lay preacher, not a proper vicar of course, one o' them 'methodicals' I think it was. 'E tried startin' a meetin' in the billet. 'E wanted to call it a Bible club an' invited us to join in, but nobody did. When the others laughed at 'im an' called 'im names, like 'Oly 'Erbert, 'e said that they couldn't see what God was like, so 'e sent 'is Son to tell us, but people still couldn't see 'cause they were blinded with sins. That made some of 'em angry, especially Billy Cragg who 'ad a very dirty mouth an' a bit of a temper."

'"So God made everything, is that what you said, you little turd. Well I reckon 'e missed a bit out when 'e made you! Somethin' went wrong if you ask me! Let's 'ave a look! Come on lads, let's 'ave 'is pants down an' check 'im out. Give 'em a little squeeze'!"'

Jacob drew a deep breath and looked away. Hannah saw the muscles of his jaw tighten and he stood silent for a moment.

'Three o' them cornered 'Erbert an' grabbed 'im,' he went on. 'It were 'ard, just watchin'. 'E didn't fight back, see, didn't even look at 'em, just turned 'is 'ead away like a sheep when a dog goes for it. They 'ad 'is trousers off an' took turns to touch 'is private parts an' they was all bawlin' an laughin', but when Craggie grabbed 'im 'e 'eld 'is throat with one 'and an' crushed 'is privates with the other an' 'Erbert made a noise like 'e was bein' strangled cause 'e was tryin' to shout out 'cause it were 'urtin' a lot. That's when a rage come over me. I jus' went for 'em, couldn't stop myself. I rushed at 'em tearin' an' punchin' an' bitin'. Course I 'ad no real chance against three of 'em, but I done some damage to 'em before they laid me out. I got this busted nose but I never felt it at the time. I was blinded wi' rage.'

Hannah looked up into Jacob's face. His memory of Herbert Biddles had disturbed and angered him.

'Why didn't 'e just shut up an' keep 'is religion to 'imself,' he said. 'Truth is, 'e asked for it! Even after 'e got roughed up 'e didn't stop! Said we all needed 'is prayers, especially Craggy, but in the end o' course they got tired o' tormentin' 'im an' even Craggy left 'im alone. We even went quiet when he knelt at 'is bedside every night. I was damned glad when we was posted an' 'e was sent off to trainin' with the medical corps 'cause I didn't 'ave to see 'im no more!'

There was a short silence, then Hannah said ever so quietly, 'Well I think he was really brave, an' I'm very proud o' your broken nose, Jacob B. Duffy!' She thought for a few moments, then she asked him, 'Do you remember when we watched them rooks flyin' 'ome an' one of 'em got left be'ind an' called out to the others, an' one turned back an' flew 'ome beside it? Do you remember?' she said, and without waiting for an answer, she went on.

'Do you think that's what 'Erbert Biddles meant when he said that God made everything to show us what 'e's like? Is God like that bird what turned back to 'elp the one what was left be'ind, an' do you think that's why someone wrote that song what we sang at Charlie Crowther's funeral, an' that God truly is the 'elp o' the 'elpless?'

Jacob pressed his cheek against her face and murmured into the curls which covered her ear, 'You do too much thinkin'. Best not to worry about such things,' but deep in his soul he was asking himself, 'Isn't this exactly why you love her so?'

Chapter Five

Life at Skein Cottage settled into an uneven routine, since Jacob wouldn't know exactly when he may be called upon to help at the farm. He didn't mind, as long as they had enough to get by, and even Hannah's help was needed when odd manual tasks which were beyond the wizardry of mechanisation would provide a few days' work.

'We're dogsbodies,' they would say, laughing. They had given up the prospect of a family long ago and Jacob had seemed happy to accept that they had been entrusted with the task of caring for one another. They were blessed with that rare contentment which might be looked upon with disdain in the hustle and bustle of city life where aspirations and ambition often leave little time for sharing true companionship. But when Jacob set off with Grip, his Jack Russell, his nets, his pegs and his ferrets, Hannah would stay behind.

'I'll catch up with the housework,' she'd say, 'you go ahead an' enjoy your mornin'. I'll see you at lunch time. Don't be late, I'll 'ave it ready by one.'

But even before noon she'd be out, looking down the valley, hoping to see him, perhaps coming home early with a couple of rabbits. She would sometimes see a kestrel, hanging on the wind over the meadow, its wings held high in a V above its body, its barred tail fanned out and its head craning earthwards as it searched the grass for prey. Jacob had told her that hawks can see a beetle in the grass from more than five hundred feet.

Suddenly, without warning the kestrel would glide away before spreading its tail like an air brake, adjust to its chosen spot with a flutter of wings before holding still once more in quivering concentration.

* * *

One morning Samuel Jamieson called at Skein Cottage. He was warden of St Peter's, the parish church in the village and although not regular church goers, Jacob and Hannah had made Samuel's acquaintance at Charlie Crowther's funeral. He was a tall, very lean man with a large head and narrow shoulders; his height seemed to be rather an embarrassment to him, so that he appeared to be permanently on the verge of tottering; he walked carefully with a pronounced stoop as though wary of bumping his head as he picked his way through a world of imaginary obstacles.

He seemed grateful when Hannah offered him a chair and he crouched into it as though apologising for monopolising the limited space in the living room. His forehead was permanently wrinkled in a worried frown and when Hannah placed a decorated tin tray on the table, Samuel sighed as though the burden of obligatory gratitude was a little too much to bear.

'Oh, dear, Mrs Duffy,' he said in a voice which wobbled its way past his Adam's apple. 'This is most kind, and unexpectantly so, but very much appreciated. Very much so.' He examined the plate of mixed biscuits which Hannah offered him, and his hand hovered over them indecisively as he made his selection. Jacob sat in silence, his mug of tea in his hand, wondering why the church warden had called and trying not to stare at him. At last Samuel began the explanation for his visit. He took a handkerchief from his trouser pocket, dabbed his mouth and cleared his throat.

'You will no doubt be aware of the passing of Mr Stubbs, that is, Hector, as we all knew him. He had served the parish and the church for more than fifty years. He was our grave digger and general maintenance man. In other words, he kept the graveyard and the church surroundings neat and tidy, as well as preparing the last resting place for many friends of the parish. There are several notable deceased personages who enjoy the tranquillity of the graveyard and its surroundings due to the dedication of Hector Stubbs.

'The vicar has asked me to find a replacement for Hector and I do hope you do not take offence or feel that in any way I am being presumptuous, but his reverence pointed out that since Cray Valley has been sold, you may have time on your hands and that you are known and respected in the village and, indeed beyond. We may therefore do well by offering you the opportunity to consider yourself as a suitable candidate for the vacancy which has sadly arisen. There is no need to give an immediate answer, unless, of course, we are faced with the regrettable problem of an unexpected passing, when we may be reluctantly obliged to try to avail ourselves of a gravedigger who might be a complete stranger to the parish.

'If I have not offended you, Mr Duffy, I would ask that you talk this matter over with your good wife, and if, in principle you would be willing to serve the church and the parish in this way, do let me know and we will discuss duties and terms.'

Hannah had sat, as had Jacob, without drinking their tea and she looked at him now, sideways, from the corner of her eye. He was nodding, thoughtful almost imperceptible nods, and that's how, at the age of fifty-two, Jacob B. Duffy became the parish gravedigger, with the responsibility of caring for the grounds of St Peter's Parish Church.

Chapter Six

The events of Jacob and Hannah's lives appeared to be unremarkable and, as time passed, they seemed to be so absorbed with each other that they would avoid any intrusion. Now and then they would see Jeremy Melville passing in his Range Rover. He would wave and drive on down the dirt road to the village, but he never stopped to speak with them and they seemed satisfied with that. The changing seasons brought short spells of casual work and once a week Jacob would cut the grass in the church grounds. Hannah liked to accompany him, and she would spend her time weeding the graves, kneeling down and reaching over to avoid standing on the sacred ground. She knew the names on every gravestone and the dates were all committed to her memory.

Jacob couldn't help worrying a little, especially when she began calling out names as though in conversation as she moved around the tombs.

'Some of these are children,' she would say. 'Come and see Rebecca. She's only four years old; she's lying quietly here in the corner under this yew tree.'

But Jacob would turn away. 'Leave 'er in peace' he'd say, and as he drew her away she'd say, 'But they're family, Jacob, and we're to look after them.'

As time passed a change came over Hannah. She seemed to be drifting into a world where he felt excluded. Time had been kind to her and she had not lost the fresh complexion, the quick, graceful movements and natural, luxurious hair which had set him dreaming when they had first met. He began to wonder if their age difference was slowly building an invisible wall of hidden regret between them. In the early days of their marriage, she had hoped for a family.

When Jacob had been found wanting, she accepted the disappointment calmly and lovingly. She had said that they ought to be thankful for one another and that they should be grateful for all the extra time they'd spend together. But he had sometimes noticed a wistful look on her face as she sat opposite him, staring into the fire on a winter's evening. One evening in early summer he had joined her and taken her hand as she looked out over the valley behind the house.

She hadn't looked at him, but said in a hushed voice, 'Just look, Jacob, the meadow's alive. It's the wind! It's settin' it all alight like coloured fire. Just look at them buttercups, an' the clover an' them dog daisies, all quiverin' an' dazzlin' in that feathery grass. When we was children, before we lost mother, me an' my sisters used to make bracelets an' necklaces from daisies, an' we'd even make a crown out o' buttercups an' we'd draw straws to see who'd get to be the queen.'

Jacob glanced at her and saw that her cheek was wet with tears. A sense of guilt and inadequacy all but overwhelmed him, as though he had somehow cheated her.

He swallowed and said, 'I'm sorry Hannah, I'm so sorry I couldn't give you what you really wanted.' She squeezed his hand.

'It weren't your fault,' she said softly. 'Don't ever think that. We done the best we could. No woman ever 'ad a better, kinder 'usband. It's just that the grass an' the wind an' all them wild flowers reminded me of when I was a little girl.' They went inside, and Hannah said, 'Don't think I fancy any supper tonight.'

'No! neither do I,' Jacob said quickly, as if he'd been thinking the very same thing. 'Two peas in a pod, that's us. Let's have a sit in the livin' room an' enjoy a quiet evenin'.'

They faced one another in a pair of ancient easy chairs with threadbare covers. Grip, Jacob's aging Jack Russell, crept onto his lap and they sat in silence, seemingly utterly content in one another's company, but each separated by their own secret thoughts, until twilight. Out in the fading light, a fox barked from far away and Grip sat bolt upright, ears pricked. He trembled with suppressed excitement as Jacob soothed him, fondling his ears. He pushed Grip gently off his knee, stood up, stretched and yawned. 'Bedtime?' he asked.

'You go on up, I'll not be far behind you,' Hannah said. 'I'll just sit here for a while longer.'

* * *

Just after midnight Hannah crept up to the bedroom, undressed in a corner, leaving her clothes draped over a chair and put on her nightgown. She held the curtain aside a little and looked out at the night. The sky was clear and the moon was high and as the wind sighed and ruffled across Lark's Drift, she thought the meadow seemed to look like restless, long ripples of water flowing down to join the river in the heart of the valley.

She sighed and whispered to herself, 'Far away, far, far away,' and although she didn't know quite what the feeling was which stirred her soul and why she wanted to stay and hold on to the sadness which she couldn't explain, she let the curtain drop, crossed the room and climbed as quietly as she could into bed. Jacob, who had been wide awake, had held his breath, straining his ears to listen to every movement, watching her in his mind's eye and wondering how this threatening sense of separation had come between them.

The following morning Hannah had risen just before dawn. As she dressed Jacob sat up in bed. 'You alright, love?' he asked.

'I'm fine, just goin' out for a look round the meadow. Won't be long.'

She took a wicker basket from the kitchen and went out into the light of the rising sun. Within twenty minutes she was back. She left the basket outside on the oak bench; it was full to overflowing with wild flowers.

As they sat at breakfast Jacob said, 'It's our day at the churchyard. Grass an' weeds grow quick this time o' year.'

They set off for the village hand in hand. The parish church was just less than a mile away.

'Nice day for a walk,' Hannah said. 'Hope you remembered the key to the shed? I need to borrow some o' them jam jars what the Women's Institute store in there.'

In her right hand she carried the basket of flowers. Somehow Jacob knew that he mustn't object or challenge her, so he remained silent. He was checking the fuel and oil levels of the mower as Hannah found an empty box and helped herself to three jam jars from a carton marked 'WOMENS INSTITUTE, DO NOT REMOVE!' As Jacob set off with the mower, she filled two jars from an open water butt and arranged a posy of flowers in each. She threaded her way through the headstones and stopped at a small plot marked with just a white marble plaque.

JOSEPH PERKS

Born 15th July 1947, Died 31st August 1949

SAFE IN THE ARMS OF JESUS

Hannah placed the jam jar carefully in front of the little memorial and said, 'There you are, my dear little one. Hope you're happy with Jesus. You were only here for but a year, an' Jesus took you away. You can tell 'im I'll be with you someday an' we'll be together jus' like we ought to be. Amen.'

Next to Joseph's little plot, his mother and baby sister who had been stillborn, lay in a grave marked with a headstone which read,

IN LOVING MEMORY OF EMILY PERKS

Born 1st May 1921, Died 5th September 1949

AND JESSICA PERKS

Born 5th September 1949, Died 5th September 1949

TOGETHER FOREVER

Hannah knelt and bowed her head, holding the jar of flowers in both hands. 'Brought you some flowers, Emily,' she said. 'Sorry to see you passed away less'n a week after your little boy, Joseph, an' you expectin' baby Jessica. Don't see no word o' yer 'usband. 'E in't buried round 'ere. P'raps that's why baby

Jessica was took away. God knows a lot more'n us. One day we'll 'ave a proper chat an' you can tell me all about it.' She placed the flowers and stood up.

Jacob paused as he followed the mower round the gable end of the church and watched as Hannah, carrying the last jar and a handful of buttercups and daisies in her basket, headed for the corner of the graveyard. He wanted to run after her and embrace her so that she couldn't get away. He wanted to tell her that what she was doing wasn't right and if the vicar got word that she was talking to dead people in the parish cemetery there'd be serious trouble and that she might even be locked up. He felt frustrated that he couldn't love her enough to make her happy. He wanted to talk properly with her and thrash things out and stop pretending that everything was alright, but he felt useless and helpless.

Hannah knelt under the yew tree which cast a sombre shadow over Rebecca's last resting place. She knew the wording on the stone and recited as she looked up into the dark tree:

Rebecca Braid
Born 1st February 1879, Died 15th March 1883
Never Forgotten

    She took a bunch of buttercups from her basket and began to weave them into a coronet. She sang softly to herself as she worked, inventing her own simple words to the old tune of 'You are my sunshine.'

You are my baby, my little baby,
You make me happy when skies are grey,
You'll never know, dear, how much I love you.
O please don't take my baby away!

She finished the wreath of buttercups and placed them on the grave .

'Don't you look pretty?' she said happily, 'but I'm not finished yet. You'll love these!'

She began to make a necklace and bracelets, weaving and tucking the flowers together skilfully. When she was satisfied, she laid them out with the coronet at the head of the grave and the other adornments where she imagined Rebecca's body may be laid.

'Now, then,' she said, 'We can be together, and we can tell one another all our secrets and I can read stories to you. Jacob will be so pleased and excited 'cause I know he always wanted a little girl.'

'Time to go 'ome, love.' Jacob stood behind her, holding out a hand.

'Not just yet,' she said sharply, 'Rebecca was askin' to meet you, She in't got a daddy an' I was tellin' 'er 'ow 'appy you'd be that we found 'er at last. She's lookin' 'er very best an' we was 'opin' you'd be pleased, so say 'ello to 'er Jacob. Say 'ello to our little one.'

Jacob bent over and took her arm. 'Come on, love, come on!'

She tried to pull herself from him.

'Let go!' she shouted, 'You're 'urtin' me! Just let go.' She crouched, sobbing over the little grave with its simple decorations, then suddenly she seized the coronet and tore it to pieces, scattering the torn buttercups across the grass. She pulled the necklace and bracelets apart and threw the shreds away.

'Jacob, Jacob,' she wailed, 'what's wrong wi' me! What am I doin'! What's 'appenin' to us!' He eased her gently to her feet and drew her close to him.

'It's alright, it's alright,' he told her, 'I'm right 'ere, I'll look after you. I'm always 'ere, Hannah, you can depend on that.'

She gave a little shudder and took hold of the lapel of his jacket. 'Can we go home now?' she asked, 'I'm feelin' really tired.'

As they walked silently together up the lane towards Skein Cottage, Jacob was desperately searching for the right words to reassure her, when she suddenly took a deep breath and spoke.

'I'm so glad that's all over. It all came creepin' up on me, bit by bit. I got to thinkin' once in a while, about 'ow nice it might 've been to 'ave a little baby an' then, before I knew it, I was tormentin' myself. As time was passin' an' my forty-sixth birthday was be'ind me, I couldn't admit to myself I wouldn't ever be a mum.' She stopped and stood still.

Jacob turned towards her and stared; she was smiling at him, her face bright and natural. He laughed with relief, picked up a stone and threw it with all his might into the distance. Then he caught her up in his arms and carried her along, spinning round and round until she kicked her feet and laughed, 'We're too old! I'm dizzy! I'm too old for this!'

He put her down, panting as he bent over. 'Whoosh,' he puffed. 'You're right, I'm too old!'

Chapter Seven

As the years passed it could be said that their life unfolded in unremarkable simplicity. They tended their vegetable patch together. Hannah would feed the chickens and collect the eggs and Jacob would go off ferreting alone since Hannah would never want to witness the death of an animal, especially one which had been so terrified by a murderous ferret that it had fled the dark safety of its burrow only to rush headlong into the net which Jacob had pegged across its bolt hole. She would leave it to Jacob to skin and prepare it for the table and only when it was simply reduced to a plate of anonymous looking joints of meat would she be prepared to handle it.

Sometimes they would go for long walks together and on fine summer days they would often take a shoulder bag with a pack of cheese sandwiches, a bottle of water and a travelling rug. In his fifteenth year, Grip, the Jack Russell was afflicted with rheumatism. He could barely keep pace with them now, yet he was determined to follow. One autumn morning they set out for Hawkshill woods in search of mushrooms and as they chatted together, the old dog fell further and further behind until they realised he was no longer with them. They turned and saw him in the distance, limping gamely after them, and Hannah cried out and ran to pick him up. When she was still twenty or thirty yards from him he sat down and waited gratefully because his strength was spent. Jacob carried Grip in the crook of his arm as a shepherd might carry a lamb and they looked for a place to stop. They spread the rug and unpacked the sandwiches and gave Grip a drink from a small enamel basin.

That evening as they sat together in the living room Grip wouldn't settle. Every so often he would get up, stagger a little, and walk around the room before returning to lie down awkwardly and painfully at Jacob's feet.

'The old boy's finished,' Jacob said sadly. 'E's been a great dog. Kep' the henhouse clear o' rats an' 'e's laid there in that open back porch night after night in all weathers listenin' for foxes. 'E could smell 'em fifty yards away, an' when 'e did e'd be out an' at 'em!'

He leaned out of his chair and fondled the dog's ears. Grip stretched one trembling leg out, lifted his head and licked Jacob's fingers.

'Wish we di'n't 'ave to grow old,' sighed Hannah. 'P'raps we ought to go up an' leave the dog in peace.'

Jacob stood up, bent down and picked Grip up as gently as he could. He laid him on the chair and arranged a small cushion under his head.

'No sentry duty for you tonight. You've done enough. You sleep there tonight, warm an' comfy.'

But they hadn't reached the door or switched off the light before Grip struggled to his feet and half jumped, half fell to the floor. Looking straight ahead he passed them, hobbled through into the kitchen and sat at the back door, staring up at the handle. Jacob laughed softly.

'Would you look at that!' he said. 'The old boy still wants to keep us safe. 'E wants to guard the house.'

He unlocked and opened the door and Grip crossed the threshold and flopped down in his usual place on an old fleece blanket in the corner of the porch. Hannah went out and stroked his head.

'Our brave, brave boy,' she said, 'We couldn't 'ave wished for a more faithful...' But she never did finish her sentence because she was choking and the words just wouldn't come out and her cheeks were wet with tears.

'Goodnight, my old friend,' said Jacob as he closed and locked the door, 'See you in the mornin'.' Jacob rose early the next day. Before dressing, he hurried down and unlocked the door. Grip was lying on his side, eyes open, ears pricked as though he was alert and listening intently.

'Grip?' said Jacob quietly, but the dog never moved. He sensed Hannah standing behind him, looking over his shoulder.

'Is he still there?' she whispered.

'No, love, he's gone. 'E i'nt there no more. 'E's gone.' He turned towards her and she crept into his arms.

'Don't want to make it any worse'" she whispered. 'No good makin' a fuss,' but he could feel her body shaking. She drew one long, shuddering breath and said, 'We can bury 'im together, can't we?'

* * *

Autumn faded into winter and fierce winds would frequently batter and thrash the house up on the hilltop so that the galvanised lid of the rubbish bin would sometimes lift and tumble across the yard. Hannah, who was a more restless sleeper than Jacob would awaken, listen intently for a moment, then draw the eiderdown over her head and wrap herself around her husband for warmth and comfort. Despite the frequent occurrence of wild winter weather, the bedroom window was never fully closed. They had both been brought up on the land and enjoyed keeping in touch with the freshness of the outdoors.

One stormy night Hannah awoke with a start. She heard the hen house door banging in the wind and the strangled squawks of terrified chickens. 'Fox! Fox!' she yelled, digging Jacob in the ribs. He leaped from the bed without a word, threw himself downstairs and snatched his shotgun from its cupboard. He fumbled two cartridges into the breech and dashed outside. The mesh gate to the chicken run hung on its hinges. He kicked it wide open, as two of his birds rushed out of the henhouse, wings flapping. One of them crashed into his legs in a blind panic while the other collided with the wire netting, fell back, and set off round the chicken run wailing and cackling in despair. The fox bolted out into the darkness like a fleeting shadow and he swung the gun, pointed and fired.

'You got 'im! You got 'im!' he heard Hannah shouting. She had followed him downstairs and cut into the yard and she was standing barefoot, looking down at the stricken fox, her nightgown billowing in the wind. Jacob hurled his gun to the ground. There was an explosion as the second cartridge discharged.

'What are you doin'?' he screamed. 'I could've killed you!' He caught her by the shoulders and shook her violently. 'Don't ever! Don't never!' he roared 'Don't never, ever! That's all! Don't ever!' He caught her roughly and crushed her in his arms until she could scarcely breathe.

'I'd die without you,' he said in a hoarse voice. 'Just wouldnt' live. Wouldn't want to.'

She didn't answer immediately because she knew there was nothing she could say. It was just that she'd wanted to help him save the chickens.

'Let's put on our coats an' shoes an' tidy up,' she said.

As Jacob shone a torch around the henhouse, Hannah counted the slaughtered birds. There were nine.

'They don't kill 'em to eat 'em,' Jacob said bitterly. 'They kill 'em because they enjoy doin' it. They ain't honest 'unters. They're just evil, murderous varmints!'

Early the next morning Jacob buried the fox. The two birds which had escaped were lying motionless against the netting of the chicken run. 'They're in shock,' Jacob said. 'They'll take some time comin' to theirselves, if they ever do.'

Hannah took his hand and said, 'When I saw the fox was shot dead, I felt sorry for 'im, but not now. not when I've seen what 'e done.'

Chapter Eight

About a fortnight later Jeremy Melville drew up in his Range Rover. As Jacob went out to meet him, he opened the rear door, leaned in and brought out a puppy.

'Morning, Mr Duffy, I wondered if you'd like to take on this little chap? I heard your Jack Russell had died and our bitch down at the farm produced a litter ten weeks ago. We were going to keep this one, but when we heard you'd lost yours, my wife thought it may be a neighbourly gesture to offer him to you.'

Jacob was overcome with a confusion of emotions. 'Why, Mr Melville,' he began.

'Jeremy, please,' said Mr Melville waving a hand. 'Call me Jeremy.' He held out the puppy. 'Deal?' he asked. 'Will you take him on?'

Jacob took the little dog carefully in both hands. 'Would you like tea, Jeremy?' he asked, feeling rather awkward, and he was relieved when Mr Melville declined.

'No, no! Needs must! Lots to do, but I'm glad you're pleased, Great breed, the Jack Russell,' and with a wave, he was gone. Hannah was in the utility room emptying the washing machine.

'Who was that?' she wanted to know.

'It was Jeremy Melville and 'e brought us a surprise.'

Hannah turned round, saw the pup and dropped the washing into her basket.

'Let me, let me,' she said holding out her hands. She held the puppy to her face and he licked her cheek. 'O, Jacob, he's just gorgeous! What shall we call him?'

Jacob thought for a moment. 'Praps we should call 'im Grip,' he suggested, 'what do you think? 'E'd certainly 'ave a lot to live up to.'

There had never been a telephone at Skein Cottage. Jeremy Melville had suggested that it would be a more convenient means of communication when there was need of their casual help at the farm, but Jacob discussed the matter with Hannah and they had decided that their privacy was too important to compromise by opening the door to contact with an intrusive outside world with its confusion and restlessness.

* * *

One spring morning after breakfast, while sitting at the table, they began to discuss what they might do that day. It was one of those days when the world seems to have suddenly awakened. The air over the meadow was flooded with the sound of skylarks and a group of brown hares had totally lost all inhibitions as they dashed in short spurts, suddenly changing direction, kicking their hind legs high in the air and leaping, one over the other, tumbling and twisting like flying acrobats. Hannah seemed to feel a surge of life, deep within her and she stood to clear the table.

'Let's feed the chickens and ferrets and lock up an' we can take Grip an' go for a walk along the river an' round Shelley's pool. Everything's so alive this mornin.'

Jacob looked at her smiling proudly. 'You look just like you did the day I first met you,' he said.

'Well, I'll soon be sixty years old!' she answered. 'I in't no spring chicken no more, but I'm glad you seem to've no regrets!'

He stood up to help her tidy up, but as she turned towards the sink she faltered, dropped the dishes she was carrying and called out his name. 'Jacob!' She fell to the floor, striking the side of her head before rolling onto her back, twitching and staring with unseeing eyes.

He picked her up and hurried into the living room. Perhaps if he sat her in a comfortable chair she'd be alright, only please God, please 'elp me! He set her down, pushing her head back against the wing of the old armchair. He stood back and looked at her. Suddenly he made up his mind. Dashing outside, he dragged his bicycle from the shed. Within 3 minutes he was in the village telephone box, dialling 999.

'Emergencies, which service do you require? Police...' He didn't wait to listen for the options. 'Ambulance! Ambulance!' he shouted desperately. 'Skein Cottage, Crayhill Farm. Name's Duffy. It's urgent! It's urgent! My wife's collapsed! Please, please hurry!'

He cycled back up the lane to the cottage. Throwing his bicycle to one side he rushed into the house. Hannah was just as he had left her except that Grip had climbed on to the chair and lay with his head on her lap. Jacob fell to his knees and raised his arms above his head.

Looking upwards he prayed, 'God, please God, 'elp me! I just don't know what to do! Please, if you're there, will you 'elp me! If I lose Hannah, God, I'll die!' He was still kneeling when the ambulance pulled up outside.

Jacob stood outside the emergency treatment room of the local hospital. He had been waiting for two hours, straining his ears to try and hear what the voices were saying on the other side of the door. At last, a young doctor came out and Jacob's heart sank when he saw the sombre expression on his face.

'Are there any other relatives?' he asked.

'No, there's no-one else,' said Jacob 'Why, what's the matter?'

The doctor reached out and laid a hand on Jacob's shoulder. 'Bad news, I'm afraid. We couldn't save her. It was a ruptured cerebral aneurism. Uncontrolled bleeding on the brain in other words. I'm so sorry.'

Jacob looked at the doctor, trying to grasp the implications of what he had said. It was as though nothing was real. The young doctor was a mere phantom, the corridor in which they stood, the hospital itself. Nothing was real because it wasn't happening. It would all come to an end soon. It would go away and everything would be as it should be. Only he must get home to Hannah.

The doctor looked at him closely and asked, 'Do you need any help, Mr Duffy? Is there anyone else at home?' Jacob looked irritated.

'No,' he said. 'I already told you, it's just me an' Hannah. 'In't nobody else. I got to be gettin' back.' He turned on his heel and left the doctor watching him as he passed through the hospital doors and out into the spring evening which was alive with the songs of blackbirds.

It was pitch dark when he arrived home at Skein Cottage. As he went inside Grip rushed towards him, leaping high to lick his face but he ignored him and went straight into the living room. He daren't turn on the light because in his heart of hearts he knew she was gone, so he drew the curtains and went and sat in his own chair, pretending to himself that she was sitting opposite to him, but even in the darkness his eyes slowly adjusted to what little light there was, and he could see for sure that her chair was empty.

* * *

Three days had passed since the sudden loss of his wife, when Samuel Jameson paid a visit. As Jacob answered the door, Samuel, whose stoop had become more pronounced over the years, bowed his head in sympathy, shaking it very slowly from side to side. He held an envelope in his left hand as he offered his right to Jacob.

'Sincerest condolences, Mr Duffy. We are deeply grieved to learn of the passing of your dear wife. Such a shock to us all, and, of course, such a loss to the parish. Only last week the vicar was saying how beautiful the graveyard is. Indeed the flowers have thrived and flourished under the care of your, er, late wife. Quite a talking point amongst the congregation.'

Jacob was still numb with the stifled grief which he couldn't express. 'Come in, Mr Jameson,' he said.

'Thank you, thank you,' said Samuel. 'Most kind. Indeed, there is a little business which I fear we need to discuss, but first things first.' They were sat at the kitchen table and Samuel laid the white envelope in front of Jacob.

He picked it up, saying 'Am I to open this, then?'

Samuel nodded. He withdrew a card decorated with Lily of the Valley and a message which read, 'With Deepest Sympathy.' He opened the card and found five ten pound notes folded inside.

'The vicar suggested that in appreciation of the quality of Mrs Duffy's care for the graveyard and her long service we should take a freewill collection and that is the result.' Jacob stared at the card and the notes laid out on the table. He cleared his throat.

'Most generous, you must thank all concerned,' he said hoarsely. 'Hannah loved keeping the graves nice. She loved it.'

Mr Jameson looked quickly at Jacob and cleared his throat nervously. 'There is one other matter which is rather delicate, Mr Duffy, and that concerns the preparations for the internment of your late, er, lady wife. It is the hope of the vicar and indeed the Parish Council that she will be laid to rest in the graveyard which she tended with such care over several years and part of the purpose of this visit is to ensure that you are comfortable with our proposal.'

Jacob sat quietly for a moment. It was as though the practical arrangements for Hannah's burial were a harsh reminder of the finality of her passing.

'She in't comin' back then, Mr Jameson,' he said simply. 'She in't never comin' back.'

Poor Samuel bowed his head and clasped his hands around a bony knee as Jacob sat quite still, staring at nothing although inwardly he was roaring in anguish.

'You said there was another matter, Mr Jameson,' Jacob said in a flat monotone.

'Ah, yes, indeed, thank you, Mr Duffy for reminding me. It concerns the actual digging of the grave. Perhaps this is not an opportune time, but the matter needs to be decided.'

Before Samuel could continue Jacob said, 'Mr Jameson, nobody will lay Hannah to rest but me. I am the one who will prepare the sacred place where she will lie but I want you to please report to the parish that this will be my last duty as grave digger.'

The frown all but disappeared for a moment from Samuel's brow, such was his relief that his painful task seemed to have been satisfactorily accomplished.

'The vicar, that is, the Reverend Crowhurst, sends his personal condolences and will no doubt visit you to discuss any readings or particular hymns you would wish to be included in the service.'

Jacob held up a hand. 'Now 'old on,' he said, 'don't ask me about no readin's. Don't know nothin' of readin's. I only 'eard that you got to look around you to see what God's made to see what 'e's like. An' I don't even know if that's what it says in the Bible. I 'eard that when I was soldierin'. An' as for hymns, I don't know any but there was one what they sang at Charlie Crowther's funeral an' I'd like that because Hannah were fair taken with it. Don't know what it's called, but it says "'elp 'o the 'elpless'" an' Hannah loved that bit.'

With a sigh of relief, Samuel Jameson said, 'Ah, 'Abide with me'! A beautifully appropriate hymn for such a gracious lady! "Help of the helpless. O, abide with me".'

Jacob nodded. 'That's the very one,' he said. 'Thank Reverend Crowhurst and ask him to kindly take charge of the service.'

On the day of Hannah's funeral Jacob rose just before daylight, locked up and set off for Shelley's pool. As he walked down Lark's Drift, Grip left the path, darted into the knee-high grass and barked in frustration as a pair of partridges took to the air with a whirring of wings, and glided together all the way across the river, alighting as the first gleam of sunlight lit up the far corner of the barley field a mile away on the far side of the valley.

Jacob stood still for a moment before saying aloud, 'You in't dead, Hannah, that'd be impossible!' He reached Shelley's Pool and sat at the water's edge. As the sun rose, he watched a hatch of olive and gold flies emerging from the pool, wriggling out of their nymph casings to stand elegantly on the surface of the water, drying their wings before joining the growing cloud which swirled and rose before spreading across the pool, under the trees and out again from the shadows into the sunlight, coming together and flying, joined as in the perfect coupling. He knew that in a few hours they would be spent. The gallant male would fall exhausted to the water while the final act of his partner would be to alight like a tiny flurry of dust to lay her eggs on the surface and they would sink into the depths of Shelley's Pool where they would hatch and live as unseen nymphs until next year, when they would rise again, just as they had done today. Suddenly he thought of Herbert Biddles and his notebook of drawings. 'What was it that Herbert used to say? "You can see what God is like from what he's made."'

He looked at his pocket watch and saw that the time was almost eleven. He must go now and prepare for the service at two-thirty. As he walked up the rise to the cottage, now and then he paused to pick a few wildflowers which he put in a jar of water, setting it on the kitchen table. He put on his best shirt and shook the dust from his only formal jacket. He looked ruefully at his fingernails. He'd done his best with them, but they were far from perfect. But people would surely remember that only yesterday he had dug Hannah's grave.

As he set out for the church, he took the flowers from the jar and wrapped the stems in damp paper. Samuel Jameson stood at the church entrance, ready to welcome mourners and show them to their seats. His shoes had been polished until they glittered and his stiff, unyielding collar made it difficult for him to turn his head.

'Ah, good afternoon, Mr Duffy, is there anything I can do for you? I am here to assist in any way I can.'

But Jacob walked past him and round the gable of the church towards the mound of fresh earth close to the stone boundary wall where Hannah was to be laid. He had placed a green tarpaulin across the open grave and secured it with heavy wooden batons, which he removed. He rolled up the cover, laid it aside and scattered the wild flowers on the dark earth in the bottom of the grave. As Samuel guided him to a seat at the front, he was unaware of the dozen or so mourners who had come to show their last respects to Hannah, who had been neither close friend nor enemy to either of them.

Jacob wondered where the Vicar had gleaned the information as he began to sketch out some details of Hannah's life. Who had told him that she had been brought up in an orphanage and had joined the Land Army as a girl of seventeen? Jacob began to feel uncomfortable as though the focus on Hannah's past was an intrusion of their privacy. He barely noticed the prayers which Reverend Crowhurst intoned in a pulpiteer's monotone in language which was confusing and unfamiliar, and he was startled when he heard his name mentioned as the one who had specially requested the final hymn, 'Abide with me.'

He stared at the hymn sheet in his hand, but the words seemed unfamiliar until he read the line, 'Help of the helpless, O abide with me!' He thought of that dreadful moment when Hannah had collapsed on the kitchen floor and lain with her face twitching and her lips moving soundlessly. He had fallen to his knees, and for the only time in his life he had called on God for help, but to no avail. The hymn ended; the organ music died away with a sigh from the ancient instrument.

The Vicar pronounced the doxology and invited the mourners to witness the interment. The pall bearers stepped forward and hoisted the coffin to their shoulders as Samuel Jameson waved Jacob from his place so that he may be the first to follow his wife to her last resting place. In his mind's eye he could see her very clearly, lying in her one and only best dress with hands folded across her breast, her face serene and untroubled, her eyes closed in a deep sleep.

The only words that Jacob remembered from the service that day were spoken at the graveside as the coffin was lowered to rest on the wild flowers which Jacob had picked that day after he had watched the hatching of the olive and gold flies at Shelley's Pool.

'Jesus said, "I am the resurrection and the life. Those who believe in me shall live, even though they die, and those who live and believe in me shall never die."' He wondered how this could be and realised that it didn't include him because he simply didn't understand what believing in Jesus really meant. He had suspected that Hannah knew something about all this, but he had always avoided discussing such things because he was afraid that they might somehow come between them.

* * *

That evening he sat in their usual place against the rear wall of the cottage. He had been hoping to see the rooks flying home but they were already gone. He felt a pressing sense of loneliness rising painfully in his chest as though seeking some way of escape, and when he could bear it no longer, he opened his mouth wide and roared in anguish. Grip leapt from his lap and scurried into the porch to settle warily on his blanket.

All at once he heard a lone rook calling loudly as though it had lost its way. He watched as it flew unsteadily westwards in the half-darkness, crying and crying as it flew home alone. He checked the ferrets' cages, secured the door to the chicken house and went into the unlit cottage where he sat in silence until the small hours of the morning.

Chapter Nine

As time passed Jacob became increasingly reclusive. His hair, which Hannah had always cut for him, grew long and matted, and his grizzled beard framed his face like a tangled rag. He had long since ignored any offers of casual work on the farm, having little need of money, but would sometimes be seen striding out across the horizon, Grip at his heel, and a bag of ferrets on his shoulder, or bent over his vegetable plot, or throwing greens over the wire fence around the chicken run.

As time went by he developed a stoop and a pronounced limp as his age took its toll on him. He would sit sometimes at Shelley's Pool and watch the male sticklebacks defending their territory and the water boatmen skimming the surface in fits and starts, leaving a perfect V in their wake. A huge sadness would sweep over him as he remembered those precious times spent down here with Hannah as they shared cheese and bread and watched the pond water coming to life. He would begin talking to her to her, asking questions she couldn't answer.

One summer morning he watched the larva of a dragonfly laboriously creeping up a reed near the water's edge. He watched, awestruck as the dingy body  writhed and struggled until at last the skin of the head burst open and the dragonfly began to emerge from the casing which had bound it fast since it had hatched from its egg two years before. At last, the wondrous creature slowly unfolded its two pairs of delicately powerful wings and revealed a golden yellow body decorated with jet black rings.

Jacob sat spellbound, scarcely breathing as the dragonfly drank in the morning sunshine, slowly flexing its wings like a fledgeling bird preparing to fly. All at once, with a sweet whirring sound the glowing creation took to the air. Something stirred in the back of his mind, words that he remembered from Hannah's funeral service, words that Reverend Crowhurst had said as the coffin was lowered into the darkness of the grave which he himself had prepared,

'Jesus said, "I am the resurrection and the life. Those who believe in me will live, even though they die, and those who live and believe in me will never die!"' He had done his best, all those years ago, to defend Herbert Biddles, who had said that people can see what God is like if they look carefully at what he's made. He knew that Hannah had believed what Herbert said and that he had been jealous because he didn't want to share her love with anyone else, but as he had watched the miracle of the new birth of the dragonfly he thought he had begun to understand just a little of what Herbert had meant.

He stood up and leaned over the water, wanting to look into the depths of the pool where he thought many secrets might be hidden. He saw his reflection staring up at him, the shaggy tangled hair, the ragged beard and the threadbare shirt with its dirty frayed collar. He stood up and tried to straighten his back as the golden dragonfly danced and whirred around his head before darting away into the trees to hunt for insects.

When Jacob arrived back at Skein Cottage that afternoon, he looked through the kitchen drawer and found a pair of scissors. Standing in front of the cracked mirror in the bathroom, he stared at a reflection he hadn't seen for many months. He shook his head, seized a large hank of hair in one hand and hacked it off, dropping it on the floor. Little by little he reduced his hair to a rough, even patch. He took a razor from a cupboard, sharpened it on a leather strap hanging from the wall, soaked his face as best he could using cold water and a dry block of green soap and shaved his beard, which came away in matted grey clumps. He had decided that God was trying to show him that there's another life which had something to do with believing in Jesus, and he ran a bath of cold water.

* * *

Early one morning Jacob heard Jeremy Melville's Range Rover pulling up at the front door of the cottage. He waited until he heard a knock.

'May I come in, Mr Duffy,' Jeremy said as he walked through the hallway into the sitting room. He had a slim document case in his hand and pointed to a chair. 'May I sit down, Mr Duffy? There's some important business to discuss.'

He deposited himself in an easy chair in which nobody had sat but Hannah since the day of his late mother's stroke. Jacob felt uncomfortable and remained standing as Jeremy opened the document case and took out several sheets of printed paper.

'These documents,' said Jeremy Melville, 'pertain to a procedure that is known as a compulsory purchase order. That is to say, Skein Cottage and the surrounding meadowland as far as the edge of Shelley's Pool have been purchased by the Department of the Environment for the purpose of providing a much-needed bypass for the village in order to alleviate the threat of heavy goods traffic which not only presents a hazard to the life of the village, but which threatens the very fabric of many of the local houses, a number of which are listed buildings.

'Now, Mr Duffy, you must be aware that you have been invited to attend a number of meetings in the village hall on this subject, and although I have personally seen to it that personal invitations have been posted through your letterbox, you have declined the opportunity to attend, so that crucial decisions have been made without your knowledge. Work on the bypass is due to begin in six weeks, which leaves little time to make alternative arrangements for your future accommodation.

'However, I am authorised by the Parish Council to offer you your own room in a retirement home only a few miles from here, which is warden controlled, and quite comfortable with a community hall where musical and tombola evenings are a regular feature, as well as plenty of opportunities to enjoy a large television screen, a communal dining hall and shared garden. Unfortunately, Mr Duffy, dogs are not permitted and since your animal is, as I recall all but fourteen years old, the kindest course of action as far as he's concerned would be euthanasia since it would be very difficult to rehome him and he would no doubt be unhappy if he was to be separated from you after all these years.'

Jacob stood motionless, unable to digest properly the implications of what he had just heard.

'I don't know what you're tryin' to do, Mr Melville,' Jacob said, 'but it don't make no sense to me. I don't know why you've written them papers up or what you're expectin' to get out of this, but I've got legal papers of my own what Charlie Crowther 'ad drawn up for me an' Hannah. I've kept my papers safe an' tidy like Charlie told me to an' this house is mine, rent free 'til I'm dead an' gone, so don't go talkin' about lockin' me up in no room an' puttin' my dog down an' destroyin' my whole entire life wi' all them memories o' my family an' Hannah my wife, 'cause they know what's goin' on an' they know why you're doin' this. An' now, Mr Melville, I'm askin' you to leave an' not come back. My shotgun's in its place. I got plenty o' cartridges, an' I in't afraid to use it!'

'Now look here, Duffy,' said Jeremy Melville, 'This is ridiculous and quite unnecessary! How old are you? Eighty two? Eighty three? You've lived rent free for all these years, and even now we've done our best for you. You really do need to see sense because there's nothing you can do! This compulsory purchase order transcends any agreement you may hold.'

Jacob didn't answer, but left the room, returning after a moment with his shotgun. He held two cartridges in his left hand and he pushed them very deliberately into the open breech. He snapped the gun shut and flicked off the safety catch with his thumb, then pointed it directly at Jeremy Melville.

'You've got just ten seconds to get out of my house a' you can take them papers with you!' he said through gritted teeth.

Mr Melville stood to his feet and said, 'Alright, Duffy, alright, but I must tell you, you are making a grave mistake.'

Jacob pointed with the gun to the door. 'You've already overstayed your welcome, Mr Melville,' he said menacingly.

'On your own head be it!' said Jeremy as he left.

Chapter Ten

Dennis 'sniffer' Shaw was delighted with his article which had been given front page prominence in *The Echo*. ARMY VETERAN GOES TO WAR, said the headline above a photograph of Jacob at an upstairs window of Skein Cottage, his face contorted with fury, his shotgun pointed at the camera. The caption read: AN ENGLISHMAN'S HOME IS HIS CASTLE.

The article was attributed to Dennis Shaw and Russ Norris, and was a sympathetic account of Jacob B. Duffy's dilemma, who, along with his faithful dog, was about to be evicted, at the age of eighty-three from the cottage in which he was born and in which he had lived all of his life, apart from the five years which he had given in active service for his king and country. There was a photograph of the protest group with their placards and a short account of the conversation with Ms Edith Sproston which included an appeal to all concerned for the environment and with the cause of justice to rally round and join the protest.

Dennis could never have dreamed that his morning's work would result in such a variety of indignant protest. On the day following publication, a rapidly growing crowd trudged up the lane from the main road to gather on the land around Skein Cottage. Half a dozen police constables were standing together around the door of the house, watching out for any signs of unacceptable activity. Ms Edith Sproston was all but overwhelmed and soon saw that she was in danger of being overlooked in the contest for attention and in fact it became clear to her that amongst the crowd were now a number of rabble rousers and anarchists. Trying her best to maintain order she raised a hand and prepared to make a speech.

'Friends and fellow protestors, let us all be clear,' she bellowed, 'We are here on a mission! We are here to do our duty. It is a duty of protection. We are here to protect our environment, the nesting sites of larks and the breeding grounds of amphibians, such as frogs, toads and newts. Yes! Newts! We are here to protect endangered native species such as the water vole, not forgetting Mr Jacob B. Duffy, a war hero and a lifetime resident of Skein Cottage who is at this moment imprisoned in his home which stands there before our eyes. In two days' time, he will be forcibly and brutally evicted, and his home, an ancient landmark, will be bulldozed and destroyed!'

Edith was now so overcome with emotion that her voice failed her. A young man with a mass of dreadlocks began to strum a guitar and sing, crouched over his instrument croaking away in a time-honoured impersonation of the standard protest singer.

'We shall overcome,' he wailed, 'We shall overcome! We shall overcome some day! Deep in my heart, I do believe, we shall overcome some day!'

Gradually some in the crowd, who had been wondering what to do, joined in.

'God is on our side! God is on our side! We shall overcome some day! Deep in my heart, I do believe, We shall overcome some day!' But right on cue, just as Ms Sproston seemed to have regained control by conducting vigorously with her right hand, a large green van came bumping gingerly up the lane.

'It's the telly!' someone shouted. 'We're going to be on telly!'

A rival group began a chant, led by an untidy young lady, who, despite her lack of bulk, was possessed of a remarkably loud voice. 'Whad'we want?' She screamed, and some of the crowd provided the required echo, although not quite sure of what it was they wanted, 'Whad'we want?' they demanded to know.

'Justice!' shrieked the skinny young lady.

'Who's it for?' the protestors yelled.

'Jacob Duffy!' came the answer. Another group seized on the name.

'One Jacob Duffy, there's only one Jacob Duffy!' they sang, adding to the mayhem as Edith Sproston desperately tried to restore order with yet another spirited rendering of 'We shall overcome.'

A cameraman was moving among the crowd, followed by a presenter who was trying to make some sense of the protest. All at once the strident chimes of an ice cream van came echoing up the lane as a resourceful vendor saw an opportunity to profit from the situation.

Chapter Eleven

Jacob B. Duffy sat in his old, winged armchair with Grip at his feet, growling non-stop, a deep, disturbing growl, as Jacob read over and over the document which Charlie Crowther had drawn up for him, and which stated his unequivocal right to the lifelong tenancy of Skein Cottage. He could trust Charlie, he told himself.

At two-thirty in the afternoon the crowd began to drift away. The truth is, there was little or nothing to do. What did it really matter if the ugly old stone cottage had to be demolished? And who was this Jacob B. Duffy anyway? Wasn't he on his last legs? He needed to be in a care home.

Edith Sproston wasn't sorry to see them go, though they had left litter—and worse, as a number of them had need to visit the gorse bushes. The anarchic element had dispersed, since there was really nothing to destroy, or even climb over. They had hoped to tempt Jacob to come out of hiding with his gun, like a tormented badger leaving its sett to face a pack of dogs, but the police presence had kept the mischief-makers at bay. The faithful few would remain until four o'clock and return tomorrow to keep vigil until the following day when the bailiffs were to carry out the eviction, supported by an armed police unit.

* * *

At around five o'clock, when all had fallen eerily quiet, Jacob left by the back door of the cottage and checked on his ferrets, before collecting the eggs in a small wicker basket from the chicken house. As he locked the door he turned towards the oak bench where he would sit until sundown, he was startled by a stranger who had walked around from the front door and who now stood looking at him.

'Is it me you want,' Jacob asked. 'Who are you?' The stranger held out his right hand.

'You don't remember me?' he asked. 'It's Private Biddles, It's Herbert, Herbert Biddles.' Jacob's eyes narrowed as he peered at the 'ghost' who stood, hand outstretched, looking steadily at him.

'Saw your picture,' he said, 'It was in the papers. I caught the train, and here I am. Got a bus from the station to Brixtock and it dropped me at the bottom of the lane. I could hear you seeing to the chickens so I just walked round. Sorry if I startled you, but I thought you might need a friend. I never forgot you, Jacob, and what you did for me and when I saw what the papers said, I heard God telling me I had to come.'

Jacob took Herbert's outstretched hand. He was all but overwhelmed by the kindness in Herbert's voice.

'It's been all of sixty years,' he said. 'Fancy you rememberin' me after all this time! An' I'll tell you what's truly a miracle, an' that is that old Grip never made a sound when you crept up on us!'

Jacob led the way into the house. 'Let me scramble some eggs,' he said. 'In't got nothin' else, I'm afraid, but I can make a pot o' tea.' The two men faced one another across the kitchen table.

'Mind if I give thanks?' Herbert asked. Jacob shook his head.

'Don't mind,' he shrugged, and Herbert closed his eyes.

'Thank you, our heavenly Father for such a wonderful day, and for bringing two old friends together to share your kindness after all these years, and thanks for these fresh scrambled eggs and for our tea and for one another, but above all, thank you for our brother and closest friend, Jesus Christ who loves us, and who gave himself for us, Amen.'

Jacob had never heard anything like Herbert's prayer and he sat with closed eyes, wondering whether or not it was finished. Herbert tactfully cleared his throat.

'Sorry,' Jacob said, 'It was like you was talkin' to a real person. I didn't want to interrupt.'

After supper the two men sat in the living room, Herbert in Hannah's chair, facing Jacob.

'So,' Jacob began, 'Did you ever marry, 'Erbert?'

Herbert seemed to wince a little before replying, 'I did, I did, but I'm afraid it didn't last. I don't think I was good enough for her though I thought I was doing my best. When I left the army I went to college and graduated with a degree. My mother persuaded me to offer for the ministry and I was appointed to a Methodist church in west Yorkshire. That's when I met Grace, a lovely Christian girl, and we were married, but she wasn't happy. In fact, I think I must have irritated her because she began acting strangely. I had a portfolio of my best drawings which a publisher wanted to prepare for a book on natural history but Grace destroyed them all. She tore them into shreds, poor girl.

'She must've been so unhappy because she left me and went away. I heard later that she was living with the organist of a large cathedral. He must have been a very talented man because, as far as I know, he was an accomplished pianist who played in a number of well-known venues. Grace asked for a divorce and I didn't object, but I never wanted anyone else. When I retired from the ministry, I moved into our family home in Norfolk. I had an annexe built and used to let it to holiday couples. It's a bit remote and looks out across the North Sea, perfect for drawing and painting. I'm afraid I stopped welcoming visitors a few years ago and I manage well enough, but I have to admit I do get lonely at times. My pension's enough for me, and now and then I'll sell a picture. But what about you, Jacob? The newspapers said that you're a widower.'

'My wife's called Hannah,' Jacob said. 'Weren't never ever a sweeter, lovelier girl. We was so close we always knew what each of us was thinkin'. She was so graceful an' light an' quick on 'er feet she made me feel awkward. All the parts o' 'er were perfect, 'er skin, 'er eyes, 'er hair, even 'er feet were beautiful, like a dancer's feet. We was never separated, not for one single day in all them years we was married. We didn't want for nothin' 'cause we 'ad each other 'ceptin' she would dearly've loved to 'ave 'ad a baby, but we still managed in spite o' that failin' o' mine.

'She were always referrin' to what you used to say about seein' God all around you, even in the birds an' flowers an' all sorts o' creatures. O, yes, I told 'er what you said, but I 'eld 'er back an' told 'er not to bother 'erself wi' no religious ideas, 'cause I were jealous, an' then one day, just when we were getting' to understand an' love each other more an' more, she fell down on the floor right in front o' me, right afore my eyes, she went down an' she never got up again. I couldn't do nothin' but call out to God to 'elp me 'cause Hannah said she thought that 'e's the 'elp o' the 'elpless like it said in the hymn at Charlie Crowther's funeral, but God din't give me no 'elp 'Erbert, 'cause she what was my angel never spoke again. She just flew away somewhere else.

'I've been on my own since then, 'Erbert an' tomorrow they say they're comin' for me to take me to some room somewhere an' lock me up, even though I've got a document what Charlie Crowther 'ad drawn up to guarantee that I can stay 'ere 'til I die. An' it seemed that nobody in the whole world really cared what 'appened to me. There's been a lot o' shoutin' an' bawlin' outside all day, but none of it really means nothin', 'cause nobody really cares. When I'm gone, they'll be gone an' start up somewhere else 'cause it don't mean nothin' an' I in't nothin' either, but I 'ave to tell you, 'Erbert, I'm intendin' to take two of 'em wi' me when they take me down!'

He pointed to the corner of the room where his loaded shotgun stood in the corner.

Herbert sat in silence for a few moments, praying for some word of comfort and grace for his suffering companion. Finally, he said quietly, 'Jesus cares.' Jacob laughed, a short scoffing laugh.

'Jesus?' he said angrily, I don't know no Jesus.'

'No, but I do,' Herbert answered. 'I know he's a real person because he sent me here today. I wouldn't 've come on my own. I saw your picture in the paper. I saw it with his eyes, not mine. I felt the pain which I saw in your face, but it was really Jesus who felt it, not me. He knew that people would make a spectacle of you, and that they'd pretend to support you and sympathise with you, and that in just a few days' time they'd have forgotten you and they'd be off making a fuss somewhere else and in a year or two cars and trucks would be roaring over the ground we're sitting on now and Jacob B. Duffy and Skein Cottage would be lost and long forgotten.

'Jesus knew all this, and his heart ached for you because he cares, and you're important to him. I know for sure that's true because he lives in me and I can feel what he's feeling. That's what it means to follow Jesus. That's what it means to be a Christian.'

'Are you talkin' about believin' in Jesus?' Jacob asked, 'cause that's what Reverend Crowhurst read out at Hannah's funeral. 'E said anyone who believes in Jesus will never really die. Somethin' to do with resurrection an' new life, like I seen 'atchin' down at Shelley's Pool. That's what convinced Hannah, but it bothered me, 'Erbert, I don't mind tellin' you, 'cause I can't forget 'ow they treated you in the army, an' that was all on account o' this Jesus o' yours! It in't easy.'

'No,' said Herbert, 'Of course it's not easy! But you've got the rage of murder in your heart, Jacob! You're in terrible trouble. They know you've got a gun; they know you're desperate. They'll clear the lane and come in an armoured vehicle. There'll be an armed police unit with high powered rifles. They'll have riot shields; they'll surround the house and they'll batter the door down. You won't survive, Jacob. In less than a week Skein Cottage will be rubble. They'll make a pile of all your furniture, your clothes, your personal things and burn it all!' Herbert pointed to a black and white wedding photograph on the sideboard. 'Just look at that beautiful girl,' he said. 'Just look at how proud you were! Who's going to care when that's burned and smashed? Of course, it's not easy, Jacob! This is your life, your whole life! My heart's breaking for you, Jacob, because I care! And I care about you because Jesus cares.'

Jacob looked at Herbert's face. It was drawn with pain and wet with tears. A strange longing swept over him. He spoke so quietly that Herbert didn't catch what he said, and after a short silence he cleared his throat and spoke.

'What can I do?'

Herbert reached out and laid a hand on his shoulder, 'Believe in Jesus,' he answered.

'But how? I don't know him. I can't just say I believe in a person I've never known! But I can see that you know him.'

Herbert said, 'Give me a minute, Jacob, I need to pray.' There followed a short silence, then Herbert spoke. 'You've got fury in your heart, Jacob, and you can't get rid of it. It's a heavy burden that you're carrying, and I know, and you know, that it's going to destroy you. Have you ever heard of the cross of Jesus?'

Jacob nodded and said, 'But I could never understand it.'

Herbert went on, 'No, like you said, it's not easy, and the best way I can try to explain is that the people of this world felt the very same rage against Jesus that you feel in your heart, but he didn't hate them, or fly into a fury. In fact, he loved them, even while they were nailing him to the cross. He asked God his Father to forgive them because they didn't understand what they were doing, exactly like you, Jacob. He carried all your rage and hatred to the cross. It was all for you, Jacob, all about you, and the only way to know and believe in Jesus is to admit that there's dreadful sin in your heart and to thank him for suffering the pain of that sin and ask him to forgive you and to live in your heart so that you can learn to follow him, and that's what it means to believe in Jesus.' The two men sat quietly for several moments while Herbert prayed silently for his friend.

All at once Jacob said, 'I want to do it! I need to do it! I in't done no prayin' before, so can I just talk in my own language?'

Herbert nodded. 'That's exactly what God wants you to do,' he said.

'Sorry, Jesus an' God in 'eaven,' Jacob began, 'but I got myself into a corner wi' no way out. I've never been a good man like 'Erbert 'ere, but I got worser 'n worser when I lost Hannah. I'm sorry for shuttin' Jesus out 'o my mind for all these years, but I can tell you can 'ear me an' that you're forgivin' me 'cause I can feel somethin' 'appenin' inside o' me an' there's a terrible weight fallin' away an' like 'Erbert said you're the very one what carried it off when you was crucified. Tell 'Erbert thanks, please God, for explainin' things 'cause they in't easy. Amen.'

The two men sat looking at one another, knowing some great miracle had happened.

'Well, that's that, then!' said Jacob, 'Who'd a thought it this mornin' when there was all that commotion an' trouble? It's like I've been let out o' prison, an' I'll try to get ready to face what's comin.'

'I've got an idea,' Herbert said, 'an idea which has come to me straight from Jesus. It explains why I'm here and why I had to see that picture that was in all the papers. I know now why I had to catch the train and come across the country to find you. You were one of Jesus the Shepherd's lost sheep, caught in a snare and he wanted to set you free, and now he wants us to care for each other, because we're brothers now. We're God's own children, so we're family and I'm inviting you to come with me to Norfolk, Jacob. You can live in the annexe I told you about where you can see the sea from your window and go for walks and there's so many birds and wild flowers that come and go with the seasons, like I told you all those years ago when we were in the army, and God knew even then that these days would come and that he would call you to be his son and we could be company for one another and even share our prayers if you like.'

Herbert held out his right hand and Jacob looked at him in bewilderment as he sat in the very room in which he had been born eighty-three years before. It seemed to him as though a door had opened into a new world and although his head was swimming with confusion, he reached out and took Herbert's hand.

* * *

The two men spent the rest of the night packing essential items into a large canvas bag, and talking excitedly about the new life they would share. Very early the following morning they walked the half mile to Crayshill farmhouse and explained their intentions to a mightily relieved Jeremy Melville.

Jeremy nodded to Herbert and said, 'Now I have met a man whom I could truly call a good Samaritan.' Jeremy promised to see to the chickens and said he knew someone who'd be pleased to take the ferrets. He promised to take them to the railway station in the Range Rover and arranged to collect them in a couple of hours.

They returned to Skein Cottage and sat quietly together, each giving thanks to God for the gift of his Spirit. Jacob said he wanted to say his goodbyes to Hannah and they walked together with Grip, the dog towards the village. Barriers had been erected at the opening to the lane and four policemen were already on duty. Ms Edith Sproston was arguing indignantly with a police officer and her depleted band of protestors were standing around in a sullen huddle.

'Sorry, Madam,' the officer was saying, 'It's a matter of public safety. We have reason to believe that there is a situation which may well involve the use of firearms. There will be no access to Skein Cottage.'

Jacob stood at Hannah's graveside.

'Remember 'Erbert,' he began, ''im from the army days. Well you'd never believe it but 'e turned up at the cottage. 'E found out I'd got in some trouble an' 'e said Jesus sent 'im to 'elp me out. It's a long story, an' I won't bother you wi' it, but I want to let you know I'm on the move. The thing is, I've found out who Jesus is an' what sort o' things 'e does. Marvellous, really, an' you was right all along. I know you believed in 'im an' I'm sorry I 'eld you back, but I got the wrong end o' the stick an' wanted you all to myself, never thinkin' we could share together. The cottage is getting' knocked down today an' 'Erbert's offered me a place in Norfolk, so I'm off, but don't think I'm leavin' you, 'cause I've found out everyone what follows Jesus is together always, an' I know we'll meet again pretty soon. 'Til then, goodbye for now Hannah, an' God bless you my love, Amen.'

When Jacob and Herbert returned to the lane the crowd had swelled and more police officers had arrived. One of the giant earth movers had started up and stood throbbing with latent power as the driver revved the engine. Jacob approached the barrier and was stopped by a policewoman.

'Where do you think you're going, can't you read?' she snapped, pointing to a NO ENTRY sign. 'Nobody's allowed up there today,' she said firmly. 'There's a dangerous situation which could well develop into the loss of life.'

All at once Jeremy Melville's Range Rover appeared, jolting down the lane. He stopped at the barrier and the policewoman made as if to allow him through.

'No, no! I've called for these two gentlemen,' he said, pointing to Jacob and Herbert. They squeezed past the barrier and jumped into the Range Rover. Jacob hurried into the cottage and collected his bag.

'Now for the train station!' Jeremy shouted. As they drove away from the cottage, three bailiffs drew up in a car followed by an open truck carrying a group of hefty men with black helmets and bulky body armour. There were several riot shields stacked up against the tailgate and each of the men was armed with a high-powered rifle. As they reached the main road the bulldozer began to move, rocking and crashing its way over the rough ground towards the lane.

'We have escaped like a bird out of the fowler's snare, the snare has broken and we have escaped,' said Herbert.

'I like that, where does it come from?' asked Jeremy.

'Psalm 124,' Herbert answered.